Is Mary Relevant?

Other Books by Titus Cranny

EPISCOPATE AND CHRISTIAN UNITY (ed.)
FATHER PAUL: APOSTLE OF UNITY
FATHER PAUL AND CHRISTIAN UNITY (ed.)
FRANCISCANS AND CHRISTIAN UNITY
JOHN XVII: AS WE ARE ONE
MEDITATIONS ACCORDING TO FATHER PAUL
ONE FOLD (ed.)
OUR LADY AND REUNION
POPE JOHN AND CHRISTIAN UNITY
POPE PAUL AND CHRISTIAN UNITY
ST. BONAVENTURE: RELIGIOUS AND SPIRITUAL LIFE (ed.)

Imprimi potest: MICHAEL DANIEL, S.A.
Father General

Nihil obstat: JOHN F. COX, Ph.D.

Imprimatur: + RUSSELL J. MCVINNEY
Bishop of Providence
May 8, 1970

IS MARY RELEVANT?

A Commentary on Chapter 8
of LUMEN GENTIUM

THE CONSTITUTION ON THE CHURCH
FROM VATICAN COUNCIL II

TITUS CRANNY, S. A.

An Exposition-Testament Book

EXPOSITION PRESS   NEW YORK

EXPOSITION PRESS INC.

50 Jericho Turnpike   Jericho, New York 11753

FIRST EDITION

LIBRARY OF CONGRESS CATALOG CARD NUMBER: 72-126366

0-682-47107-0

To

SISTER GABRIEL, S.A.

of the Atonement

and

of the At-one-ment

CONTENTS

PREFACE

Relevancy is the key word today. It may not be tomorrow, but today it is "in." Everything and everyone is measured by its limits. The Apollos, the flights into space, the ABM program, are considered relevant because they have meaning for man.

Religion too finds its measuring stick in these terms. Is the Church—or are the churches—relevant? Are the structures of the past simply outmoded or must they be cast aside altogether? What does religion mean to the youth of our country? Of the world? What about ecology and Christianity?

More concretely we may ask: Is the teaching of Christ functional in the life of man today as he celebrates his journey to the moon and plans new conquests of space in the future? What does the Trinity mean to men today? Or—the point of this book—what of Mary of Nazareth? Is she relevant to the Church as she has been in the past? Is veneration of her a relic of the past with no importance for modern man—or for the man of the future? Was she a biological necessity for the Incarnation of the Word but no more than that—now to be placed on a pedestal as a museum piece?

The subject of Mary is not wholly academic. At the present time almost every point of Christian teaching is undergoing scrutiny and assessment, not for the sake of denial but for deeper appreciation, and so with the Virgin Mary. Her role is being questioned—in the life of her Son, in the life of the Church, in the economy of salvation. But to the question, Is Mary relevant? I answer, emphatically with a full heart and with unquestioning conviction, Yes!

To show Mary's relevance I have chosen to study and to explore the definitive statement of Marian teaching from Vatican Council II, given in chapter 8 of the dogmatic Constitution on the Church. The Constitution is possibly one of the most important documents presented by the Church in a thousand years and is a singular and striking contribution to its theology. Chapter 8, "The Role of the Blessed Virgin Mary, Mother of God, in the Mystery of Christ and the Church," partakes of this significance and is a most important synthesis of Marian teaching for members of the Catholic Church and for other Christians.

As Pope Paul VI noted in his letter to the Fifth International Mariological Congress at Lisbon in August of 1967: "Although it refrained from establishing any new basis for Marian doctrine, the Council nevertheless made such excellent and clear statements concerning the most Blessed Virgin Mary that we can say that it has opened new avenues of approach both for a more profound theological study and for the promotion of a sounder and healthier Christian piety toward the Mother of God."

As chapter 8 unfolds, Mary is a model of faith, of love, of union with Christ. She is the head of the communion of saints, the mother of all mankind. She has a special role in the mystery of salvation in the saving work of Christ and a special role in the great modern movement toward Christian unity—ecumenism. The theology of Mary is central to unity, for though in the hierarchy of religious truths it is subordinate to such mysteries as the Trinity and the Incarnation and Redemption, still it impinges on many beliefs of Christianity, and moreover, it elucidates from a human perspective the concepts of Christ and the Church, the communion of saints, grace and merit, and the eternal destiny of all believers.

Pope Paul has frankly admitted that Marian doctrine and practice may have constituted and may presently constitute a barrier to Christian unity. "This holy and blessed name of Mary," he said in the apostolic letter *Signum Magnum* (May 13, 1967), "has become, in a certain sense, like that of Christ, a *Signum cui contradicetur,* a sign which shall be contradicted." Still, he added, "In the last few years the Marian controversy has become calmer in tone, more doctrinal in content, and as an objective doctrine to which all the faithful must adhere, offers the light, the measure, and the joy of our veneration of the Mother of Christ." And during his historic pilgrimage to the Marian shrine at Fatima, Portugal, at the same time a journey made in the name of peace in the world and peace in the Church, the Pope greeted the group of "brother Christians" present with a specially worded welcome—

> In the present state of a divided Christianity, you do not share, brothers, all of our convictions regarding Mary. But we have her nevertheless in common as a model of faith and humility, both of which we must in our turn translate into our lives in the service of our Lord. And we may legitimately hope that together with the help of the Lord this common service will bring us nearer together.
>
> We associate ourselves, therefore, with all our heart at Mary's hymn of joy and gratitude: "My soul magnifies the Lord and rejoices in God my Saviour. . . . He has done great things for he . . . His mercy is from age to age to those who fear Him."
>
> Please accept, dear brothers, our good wishes and partake of our desire and our hope that one day we may rejoice in perfect oneness in the same faith and the same charity of all who are honored to bear the name of Christian.

Then, stressing the relation between the Blessed Virgin and the Church, between Mariology and ecclesiology, and the significance of both disciplines for our age, the Pope added—

> What a delusion our efforts to arrive at universal unity would suffer, if we fail to offer to our Christian brethren, at this moment divided from us, and to the rest of humanity which lacks our faith in its clear-cut authenticity and in its original beauty, the patrimony of truth and of charity, of which the Church is the guardian and the dispenser. We want to ask of Mary a living Church, a true Church, a united Church, a holy Church. . . .

Many decades before Pope Paul's visit to Fatima or before Vatican Council II, this same relation between Mary and Christian unity was clear to the mind and heart of Paul James Francis, S.A., founder of the Society of the Atonement at Graymoor, Garrison, New York. He originated the Unity Octave, or Week of Prayer for Christian Unity (Jan. 18–25), in 1908, just one year before the Society made its corporate entrance into the Catholic Church. Father Paul honored Mary as the special patroness of Christian unity and insisted that after Christ himself she was directing the ecumenical movement. The modern effort toward ecumenism on the part of many Protestant churches began in 1910 at Edinburgh with the Missionary Conference at which Bishop Charles Brent was a leading figure.

Father Paul venerated Mary under the title of the Atonement (which he liked to divide to form At-one-ment) and with Church approval celebrated the feast of Our Lady of the Atonement on July 9. Together with Mother Lurana Mary Francis, S.A., foundress of the Graymoor Sisters, he promoted love of the Virgin Mary through the Rosary League, begun in 1901, and through his writings for more than forty years. He preached often about Mary's role in Christian unity and always asked for prayers to her during the Unity Octave. For him Mary was the model of man's union with God and she prays with the accents of her Son for the fulfillment of the prayer "that all may be one." Mary is the type and figure of the Church on its pilgrim way; she is the Mother of faith, constantly interceding for the welfare of Christians and for all mankind.

I share Father Paul's conviction of Mary's role in the mystery and fulfillment of Christian unity. It is in this spirit that I offer my comments on this important document from the Vatican Council. I wish to stress the relevance of Marian teaching today, as well as to consider the areas of difficulty and of disagreement which emerge from the text of chapter 8. I find the thought that Pope Paul conveyed to the Carmelites at Aylesford, England, especially fitting: "We desire that pilgrims of all faiths and not the least those oppressed by doubt, indifference, skepticism, and prejudice may find their way to the sanctuary of Aylesford so that they might pray together, discuss their mutual problems and work on the protection of Our Lady, Mother of the Church, for true religious union in Christ Jesus" (July, 1965).

I believe that Mary is of a very special relevance at the present time, to give a proper dimension to the life and activity of her Son and to the purpose of the Church in human society, as the model and the mother for all mankind. As the Holy Father has stated: "Mary should always have a special place in our profession of religion, the place which is rightfully hers in the divine plan of our redemption. Her role is not one in competition with that of Christ, but one which completely depends upon and derives all from Christ, a role marvelously associated to that of Christ."

I recall too the words of Hilaire Belloc—

> Prince Jesus in mine agony
> Permit me broken and defiled
> Through blurred and closing eyes to see
> A female figure with a child.

I think that this "female figure with a child" will be with us for a long time to come.

My commentary is divided into chapters corresponding to the sections, or subchapters, of chapter 8 of the Constitution, and my headings are those used as sectional captions within chapter 8. I have used, with permission, the translation prepared under the editorship of Rev. J. Joseph Gallagher and Rev. Walter Abbott, S.J., including their documentary notes but changing the enumeration.

My commentary seeks to be ecumenical in form; that is, while relying on Catholic sources among the popes, the fathers of the Church, and theologians, it will also make use of the comments and insights of Orthodox, Anglican, and Protestant authors. Wishing to present my remarks in an expository way, not argumentative or polemical, I have relied somewhat on the thought of various Protestant scholars and authors as well as of Catholics to show the contemporary Christian mind with regard to the Blessed Virgin. There is frequent reference to Pope Paul, not so much to give a final answer to the question as to show the official teaching of the Church at the present time. I have tried to steer a middle course between statements about Mary that are poetical and exaggerated and statements that would denigrate her role in the mystery of the Christ and in the mystery of the Church.

—TITUS CRANNY, S.A.

Feast of Our Lady of the Atonement
July 9, 1969

1

THE ROLE OF
THE BLESSED VIRGIN MARY,
MOTHER OF GOD,
IN THE MYSTERY OF CHRIST
AND THE CHURCH
(52-54)

Preface to Chapter 8
Lumen Gentium

52. Wishing in His supreme goodness and wisdom to effect the redemption of the world, "when the fullness of time came, God sent his Son, born of a woman, . . . that we might receive the adoption of sons" [Gal. 4:4-5]. "He for us men, and for our salvation, came down from heaven, and was incarnate by the Holy Spirit from the Virgin Mary."[1] This divine mystery of salvation is revealed to us and continued in the Church, which the Lord established as His own body. In this Church, adhering to Christ the Head and having communion with all his saints, the faithful must also venerate the memory "above all of the glorious and perpetual Virgin Mary, Mother of our God and Lord Jesus Christ."[2]

53. At the message of the angel, the Virgin Mary received the

[1] *The Creed in the Roman Mass*: *The Constantinopolitan creed*: *Mansi*, 3, 566. Cf. *Council of Ephesus*: *Mansi*, 4, 1130 (as well as *Mansi*, 2, 655, and 4, 1071); *The Council of Chalcedon*: *Mansi*, 7, III-6; and *The Council of Constantinople II*: *Mansi*, 9, 375-96.

[2] *Canon I of the Roman Mass*. (The present version is slightly different: "We honor Mary, the ever-virgin mother of Jesus Christ our Lord and God.")

Word of God in her heart and in her body, and gave life to the world. Hence she is acknowledged and honored as being truly the Mother of God and Mother of the Redeemer. Redeemed in an especially sublime manner by reason of the merits of her Son, and united to Him by a close and indissoluble tie, she is endowed with the supreme office and dignity of being the Mother of the Son of God.[3] As a result she is also the favorite daughter of the Father and the temple of the Holy Spirit. Because of this gift of sublime grace she far surpasses all other creatures, both in heaven and on earth.

At the same time, however, because she belongs to the offspring of Adam she is one with all human beings in their need for salvation. Indeed, she is "clearly the mother of the members of Christ . . . since she cooperated out of love so that there might be born in the Church the faithful, who are members of Christ their Head."[4] Therefore she is also hailed as a pre-eminent and altogether singular member of the Church, and as the Church's model and excellent exemplar in faith and charity. Taught by the Holy Spirit, the Catholic Church honors her with filial affection and piety as a most beloved mother.[5]

54. Therefore, as it clarifies Catholic teaching concerning the Church, in which the divine Redeemer works salvation, this sacred synod intends to describe with diligence the role of the Blessed Virgin in the mystery of the Incarnate Word and the Mystical Body. It also wishes to describe the duties of redeemed mankind toward the Mother of God, who is Mother of Christ and Mother of men, particularly of the faithful.[6]

The synod does not, however, have in mind to give a complete doctrine on Mary, nor does it wish to decide those questions which have not yet been fully illuminated by the work of theologians. These opinions, therefore, may be lawfully retained which are freely propounded by schools of Catholic thought concerning her who occupies a place in the Church which is the highest after Christ and yet very close to us.[7]

---

[3] The foundation of all Mary's other privileges is her dignity as mother of the Son of God.

[4] St. Augustine, *De s. virginitate*, 6: PL 40, 399.

[5] The Council comes very close here to calling Mary "Mother of the Church." This title, while not bestowed by the Council itself, was actually conferred by Paul VI in his closing allocution at the end of the third session, Nov. 21, 1964.

[6] This paragraph succinctly states the purposes of the whole chapter.

[7] Cf. Paul VI, allocution to the Council, Dec. 4, 1963: *AAS*, 56 (1964), p. 37.

Chapter 8 of the Constitution on the Church is a compendium of Catholic teaching on the Blessed Virgin Mary. It is the longest statement on the Blessed Virgin ever to emanate from any general council. It is a positive exposition to which appeal can be made alike in the face of either exaggeration or belittlement of Mary's place in the divine plan of elevation. It is also important for ecumenical development. For many Christian brethren of other churches have felt that the definitions, for example, of the Immaculate Conception and of the Assumption drove deeper the gulf between them and the Catholic Church that so honors Mary.

In style and tone this document is like the other documents from the Vatican Council, with a heavy reliance on Scripture, the Church fathers, and simplicity of expression. They are different, for example, from the form of expression of the definition of the Immaculate Conception in 1854 and the definition of the Assumption in 1950. This chapter, composed of eighteen paragraphs, is about 3,500 words in length.

Within a week before the close of the first session in December, 1962, the question arose which of the two schemata should be discussed first: that on the Church or that on the Blessed Virgin. It did not seem worthwhile to plunge into the formidable schema on the Church; the Marian schema, much shorter, seemed to stand a reasonable chance of being accepted, even with modifications. And from a devotional point of view, it seemed fitting to publish the decree on the Feast of the Immaculate Conception, December 8, the date on which the first session was due to close (the Council had begun on the feast of the Motherhood of Mary, Oct. 11). The Council fathers, however, decided to initiate discussion on the Church, and so there was more time for a thorough and critical examination of the Marian schema during the ensuing session.

A more important matter for decision was the question whether the schema on the Blessed Virgin should be separate from the schema on the Church or incorporated within it as was intended during the preparatory period. It was not a question of Mary's being more honored or less honored: devotion

to her has always had a secure place in Catholic piety. The
question was: Which is the better way to explain Mary's position in Catholic thought and devotion? Should she be treated
as a figure apart, or in a context that would bring out her role
in the work of redemption? Those who sought to include Mary
in the schema on the Church were also concerned to maintain the ecumenical approach that the Council had taken from
the beginning.

The theological commission had carried into the plenary
session two different positions on Mariology. Cardinal Franz
Koenig of Vienna had articulated the view of those who desired that there be no separate schema about Mary but that
the text on the Mother of God should be incorporated into
the text on the Church—

> The Church is the central theme of this Council. Hence the doctrine
> on the Blessed Virgin Mary belongs in the schema on the Church,
> so as to illustrate the close connection between the doctrine on the
> Mother of God and the other parts of dogmatic theology, and
> even that certain theological concepts are not used in the same
> sense in the two fields, thus preparing the way for exaggerations
> having no theological foundation. Such objections could be solved
> more readily and more satisfactorily if the doctrine on the Blessed
> Virgin Mary were included in the schema on the Church. Mary on
> earth cannot be passed over in silence. Thus each of these doctrines
> complements the other, and the whole of our eschatological doc-
> trine and the whole of our Mariological doctrine complete each
> other. If the Church were only an institution of salvation, then the
> Blessed Virgin Mary could be outside. But since the Church is the
> people of God and a community of saints, the Blessed Virgin
> Mary must be in this schema as an eminent member of the People
> of God.
>
> Mary as a fruit of the Redemption is an eminent member of
> the Church and typically is also a means of salvation, passing on
> to others what she herself received entirely from Christ. Thus,
> since the Church, as a fruit of Redemption, is also a means of sal-
> vation, the doctrine on the Church and on the Mother of God will
> be better explained together.
>
> No one wants to obscure or lessen the dignity of the Blessed
> Virgin Mary. No one aims to describe her role in the Church in
> any way which would make her only one member among many,
> passively receiving the benefits of Redemption. Since the Church

is not merely a fruit of Redemption, but an instrument of Redemption, wielded in the hand of Christ and cooperating actively in salvation, the Blessed Virgin Mary can best be set forth as a most exalted Co-operatrix with Christ. [Sept. 29, 1963.]

The theological commission of the Council had earlier prepared a text entitled "The Blessed Virgin Mary, Mother of God and Mother of Men," but this had not come up for debate formally during the first session of the Council. The Marian question was, in fact, first discussed in the debate on the Church. This discussion began at the end of the first session (Dec., 1962), and as it continued into the second session it became clear that a definite trend was emerging that favored including the schema of Mary in the schema on the Church. To clarify this situation a confrontation of Cardinal Santos of Manila and Cardinal Koenig took place on October 24, 1963, early in the second session, to put before the fathers of the Council the points for and against the inclusion. By the historic vote of October 29, 1,114 bishops voted in favor of the inclusion and 1,074 voted against it. By a mere 40 votes the Council of 2,300 bishops decided that their statement on Mary would form part of their statement on the Church. This was a procedural decision, but it had clearly important theological implications.

Bishop Christopher Butler, O.S.B., auxiliary bishop of Westminster (England), abbot of Downside Abbey at the time of the Council, admitted that much thought, prayer, and even anguish went into the discussion about Mary. "It must be conceded," he noted, "that this decision and the contents of the resulting chapter cause a great deal of heart-burning. I can only say that I personally believe that devotion to Our Lady will gain in quality through the Council's resolution to 'contain' Marian doctrine within the framework of the theology of her Divine Son and of the Church of which she is both type and 'pre-eminent member.' "

Father George Florovsky, Orthodox theologian, put it: ". . . to ignore the Mother means to misinterpret the Son. On the other hand, the person of the Blessed Virgin can be properly understood and rightly described only in a Christological setting and context. Mariology is to be but a chapter in the treatise on the Incarnation, never to be extended into an independent treatise. . . . There must be a Mariological chapter in the treatise on the Church."

Of course, the press had a field day. "A startling headline greeted us this morning in the daily American English language paper of Rome," Bishop Charles Helmsing of Kansas City, Missouri, wrote to his faithful. "It read: 'Prelates De-emphasize Mary.' I am afraid that similar headlines might have greeted you in our own dailies in the United States." Then he explained why he and 1,113 other bishops had voted to keep the schema on Mary in the Constitution on the Church. "As has been said repeatedly, the purpose of the council is a pastoral one; that is why Pope John called it originally; that is why Pope Paul reconvened it this past September. My vote and, I am sure, that of the other Fathers who voted for including the schema on Mary in the schema on the Church came from our desire to present in focus Mary's position in both the history of salvation and the work of salvation which is the task of the Church today."

Yielding to none, as he put it, in the love and honor which we owe Mary as the Mother of God and our mother, Bishop Helmsing continued—

> Often in singing her praises the official prayers of the Church have quoted the official words of the Old Testament which we apply to Mary: "Thou art the glory of Jerusalem, thou art the joy of Israel, thou art the honor of thy people." These words bring to our attention Mary's unique place among the people of God. Since our current discussion has been extensively on the People of God, a true and meaningful title of the Church, it is fitting that we do not exclude Mary, who has such a unique place in the Church precisely because she mothered the Son of God, the Savior of the world.

The theology of Mary, he emphasized, was "contained" in the mystery of the Church—

By basing our thinking about Mary, and above all our devotion to her on the solid foundation of divine revelation as found in our Bible and in the constant teaching of the early Fathers of the Church, we nourish in the best possible way our piety towards the Mother of God and our Mother and make it possible to converse with or have dialogue with our fellow Christians.

On this last point, wrote the Bishop:

As I see it, there is no question of minimizing the place of Mary to win over our separated brethren. Here at the council we have some of the greatest theologians among them, most of whom know our Catholic teaching and theology as well as we do. They would be the first to sense any insincerity or whittling down of Catholic doctrine for the sake of the reunion of Christendom and they would despise us for it.

In placing the treatment on Mary in our treatment on the Church, we hope that under the guidance of the Holy Spirit, we will be enhancing rather than lessening devotion to Mary.

All devoted children of Mary need not fear that the ecumenical council will deprive them of their Christian heritage in regard to the honor and love we owe Mary. They must continue to acknowledge their dependence on her as God planned; they must regard her lovingly as their advocate and helper in all their needs; they must, above all, strive to imitate her wonderful galaxy of virtues, and in particular her marvelous faith and her boundless love for God and for her fellow men.

And so felt many other bishops among those who voted to include Mary in the schema on the Church.

Between the second and third sessions an immense amount of work was done to produce a new text that would meet the wishes expressed by representatives of the two tendencies in the Council. When on March 7, 1964, the fifth successive draft came before the theological commission in duplicated form, it was further amended, and then printed at the end of the month. It was examined in more detail during the first days of the June following, and further amended. The final text went into print at the beginning of August, and carried a new and definitive title: "The Blessed Virgin Mary, Mother of

God, in the Mystery of Christ and the Church." It was on the basis of this text that the observations of the bishops to be made in the following session were prepared.

The chapter on the Blessed Virgin came up for debate at the start of the third session, on September 16 and 17, 1964. There were thirty-three episcopal interventions, and from them emerged the persisting divergence of view among the fathers which even the most worked-over schema had not succeeded in eliminating. The French Mariologist René Laurentin characterized one group as insisting on the inclusion of certain formulas and titles, that is, those already accepted and used in papal documents, and the other group as resolved to escape from these formulas, while incorporating in the Constitution their essential content.

Perhaps the most significant intervention in the debate was that of Archbishop Frings of Cologne, who spoke in behalf of more than seventy bishops. In effect, he appealed to the people on both sides to give the text the necessary two-thirds majority—which it appeared at one stage it would not get—even if voting for approval involved them in abandoning some personal Mariological viewpoint. After the amendments proposed by the fathers in this debate had been studied by the theological commission, the document, amended according to these suggestions, came again before the Council on October 29, 1964 a year to the day after the decisive vote on inclusion. The voting was: approval, 1,559; non-approval, 10; qualified approval, 521. The text was again amended and finally adopted on November 19.

A little more than a year after the vote of 1963, in November, 1964, chapter 8 was passed by 2,096 votes to 23, and in the final vote on the whole Constitution on the Church the opposition had shrunk to 5. The schema was promulgated two days later on November 21, 1964, and at the same time the Pope proclaimed Our Lady Mother of the Church.

This proclamation met with a variety of reactions, from the enthusiasm of the old Catholic countries Italy, Spain, and Portugal, to some reserve in ecumenically conscious Germany and to strongly unfavorable reactions from some non-Roman Christians who felt the gesture somehow a hostile one. But if we examine his actions and statement relative to the Marian chapters, we see that Pope Paul was clearly trying to achieve some sort of balance.

Although chapter 8 was itself a compromise, worked out over a long period, and although it was finally approved by an overwhelming majority of the fathers, the Pope seems to have felt that by itself it did not fully reflect the Mariological situation in the Church. The combination of dogmatic Constitution and formally proclaimed title of Mary as Mother of the Church seems to have suggested itself to the Holy Father as the way in which he could best give expression to what was factually there in the belief and piety of the faithful.

The proclamation was in line with the theology of the of the Marian movement, already so developed under Pius XII. It was an attempt by the Pope to meet those who were still thinking in terms of the previous popular Mariology of titles.

There has been, and with marked emphasis, a redirection of theological study of Mary, a reintegration of Mariology with ecclesiology, writes Bernard Cooke of Marquette University—

> Increasingly, the mystery of Mary is seen to be part of the mystery of the Church. Her role, her grace, and her person are studied in relation to the wider community of the faithful. Mary is viewed not as a mystery apart, as if she were parallel to the mystery of Christ as object of the Church's devotion and study, but as part of the mystery of the Church itself. Mary is seen to be within the Church the perfect Christian, the exemplar of Christian sanctity, prayer, and activity.

Father (now Cardinal) Jean Danielou, S.J., points to the Church's teaching on Mary as being of special prominence—

> The place of the Virgin Mary in Christian faith is actually one of the most difficult, most delicate and most discussed. On the other hand we feel sure, deep down in our hearts, that the place of the Madonna in the history of salvation and our love for her

constitute a touchstone of our Catholic faith. Anything that would give offence in this matter would strike something essential in us. [*Oss. Romano,* Aug. 10, 1968.]

Romano Guardini has said of the mysteries of the Christian religion, "Love does these things—and what right have we to limit this sovereign freedom of love?" We may apply the thought in a special way to God's dealings with Mary, who by Him was filled with grace and given a special role in the salvation history of the world.

The holy and simple Pope John XXIII, who won the hearts of all men during his short reign, wrote warmly and often of love for the mother of God and the Mother of men. His words are filled with light and clarity—

The Son of God, Word of the Father "without whom was not anything made that was made" [John 1:3] in the order of creation, in this mystery takes on human nature and becomes a man, in order to save and redeem all men, all mankind. When Mary Immaculate, the finest and most fragrant flower of all creation, said in answer to the angel's greeting: "Behold the handmaid of the Lord" [Lc. 1:38] she accepted the honor of divine motherhood, which at that moment was realized in her. And we, born once in our father Adam, formerly the adopted sons of God, but fallen from that high estate, are now once more brothers, adopted sons of the Father, restored to his adoption by the redemption, which has already begun. At the foot of the cross we shall all be children of Mary, with the same Jesus whom she has conceived today. From today onwards she will be the Mother of God [*Mater Dei*] and our Mother [*Mater nostra*] too.

What sublimity, what tender love in this first mystery! When we reflect on this we see that our chief and constant duty is to thank the Lord who deigned to come to save us and for this purpose made Himself man, our brother man; He has joined us by becoming the son of a woman and by making us, at the foot of the cross, the adopted sons of this woman. He wanted us, who were the adopted sons of His heavenly Father, to be the sons of His own Mother.

The Marian chapter reflects the Council's desire for integration. It is not Christocentric or "ecclesiotypical," as some people would like to call it. There is no conflict between Mary as the archetype of the Church and in her relation to Christ.

She is the archetype of the Church precisely because of her connection with Christ as His mother. Likewise, a Christocentric view of Mary is incompatible with an individualistic concept of Christ and His work. It must consider Christ together with that mysterious body which He acquired through His redemption and of which Mary is the mother and the preeminent and perfect member. Jesus is the center of the universe, "for all things have been created by Him and for Him." But the light of the world gives glory to her who bore Him, who nursed Him, who loved Him beyond the capacity of any mother or any creature, who listened to His every word and watched His every gesture, who suffered keenly because of His love, for men are her children too. Mary's role in the incarnate life of her Son cannot be ignored or minimized. As Pope Paul has declared, "The sacred synod has the deliberate intention of throwing light on the Blessed Virgin's function in the mystery of the Word made flesh and of the Mystical Body."

Chapter 8 is not immediately concerned with Mary's special graces and privileges—her Immaculate Conception, her Assumption, and the others. It concentrates on what is the source of all her graces: her place in Redemption. It deliberately directs attention to that point, which commands all the others. From its authority, as the expression of the Council, the document is of very great significance, both for Catholics and for other Christians.

Mary stands as the formal negation of every success and power of man, the complete opposite of man who seeks to reach God by his own effort. Mary is the negation of any religion that seeks to place its confidence in purely human virtue and strength for following the Law of God. In her poverty and openness Mary is a sign of the power, the grace, and the love of God, who alone can save man. Mary is a living proclamation of the mystery of grace and the benevolence of God which always predestines, precedes, and prevents us before anything good can emerge from the human heart. In her humble poverty, as mother of the *anawim*, and in her unique election, Mary is the most perfect expression of the all-

powerful and full sufficiency of divine grace. Mary's role does
not contradict the statement "to God alone be glory" but sup-
ports it and fulfills it. Mary is the most perfect expression and
testimonial of this principle. Mary does not constitute a denial
of the teaching of Scripture that there is but one mediator but
stands as a sign, as testimony of its validity. Among all the
redeemed, among all the members of the Church, Mary is the
most sublime, peerless human being, the first and the most
excellent fruit of the Redemption.

In the mystery of the Incarnation of the Word and in His
work of salvation, Mary is the principal figure after Christ.
Mary's history of her life is a revelation of God. It is part
of divine teaching; it is a tangible, visible, historical account
and aspect of God's love for man, depicted in the figure and
form of the Virgin of Nazareth. Mary's significance can be
understood only if we consider her human acts that enter into
salvation history.

The caption of the chapter is itself significant. It declares
that the basic doctrine of the Virgin Mary is "Mother of
God," defined in 431 by the Council of Ephesus, at which
Cyril of Alexandria was prominent as legate of Pope St.
Celestine I. The title from Vatican II honors Mary for her
role "in the mystery of Christ and of the Church." She is
inseparable from her Son, for all her glory is derived from
Him. She is the associate of Christ, *Alma socia Christi,* for
she shared in the mystery of salvation in a special, unique
way. She continues to share in the saving work of the Church,
as the Constitution on the Liturgy has stated.

This terse statement expresses the inseparability of Mary
from Jesus in the plan of salvation: "In celebrating this an-
nual cycle of Christ's mysteries, the holy Church honors with
special love the Blessed Mary, Mother of God, who is joined
by an inseparable bond to the saving work of her Son. In her
the Church holds up and admires the most excellent fruit of
the redemption and joyfully contemplates as in a faultless
model, that which she herself wholly desires and hopes to
be." (Art. 103.)

Thus the Marian chapter of the Constitution on the Church reveals the place of the Blessed Virgin in contemporary theology. Firmly based on the teaching of Scripture of the Church fathers, and of the popes, it keeps an admirable balance between exaggeration on one hand and belittlement on the other. For the Blessed Virgin derives her dignity, her power and her greatness from her Son as their unique source as she proclaimed in the Magnificat: "He who is mighty has done great things for me."

Chapter 8 is an integral part of the Constitution on the Church. In the last document of major importance on the Church, the encyclical *Mystici corporis* (1943) of Pope Pius XII, the section on Mary was simply an "epilogue," or appendix. There was indeed a change of emphasis between 1943 and 1964. Even in Marian devotion it would seem that there was unprecedented escalation from 1950 to 1958, and the trend promised to continue. The simplicity of Pope John placed restraint on such efforts; the tendency to isolate Our Lady and to multiply titles in her honor began to turn in another direction. At one time much writing and discussion was devoted to such distinctions as subjective and objective redemption and to such Latin phrases as *de congruo* and *de condigno;* but these terms are not even mentioned in the Marian chapter from the Constitution on the Church. Love of Mary is essential and integral to the Christian life; but it must not consist principally in extolling her privileges as if she were completely apart from the human race and apart from theology; nor does it consist in relegating her to the role of just another creature on this earth. Both extremes must be avoided; Mary must be seen and appreciated in the whole context of salvation history.

According to Pope John's famous purpose for the Council, "to let the air in," this Marian chapter seeks to integrate Our Lady anew in Scripture, the Church fathers, and the great traditions of the liturgy. It sets forth her place in God's plan of salvation. She stands in relation to her divine Son, to the life of the Church and to each Christian as, above all, the mother of the Redeemer, Mother of God. The title Theotokos, "Mother of God," is a keynote of chapter 8 and under one form or another constantly recurs. Since the Son whom she bears as man is God, she is the Mother of God. The Eastern Catholic and the Orthodox in their great devotion to Mary contemplate her chiefly under this title.

The Council teaching is given in four sections: the position of the Blessed Virgin in the plan of salvation; the role of Mary and the Church; the veneration of Mary; and Mary as the sign of created hope and comfort to the pilgrim people of God. The very captions of these sections show the restraint with which the Council fathers approached their subject. Mary is firmly placed within the saving plan of God, completely dependent on her divine Son.

It is further significant that the references given in the footnotes of the original Latin of chapter 8 abound with the names of Greek fathers, such as Irenaeus, Epiphanius, Andrew of Crete, and John of Damascus, and thus express the common devotion of East and West for the Mother of God. But above all, the exposition of Mary's place in the history of salvation and of the Church is firmly based on Scripture. This chapter is a balanced biblical and patristic exposition of doctrine on the Mother of God which has the authority of a general council. While it preserves all that is of faith, it makes openings for dialogue among Christians.

As Pope Paul observed May 29, 1968—

> The Council had no wish to expound new doctrines concerning Mary, just as it did not aim to say everything possible about her; but it did present Mary most holy in such a way and with such titles that everyone who is faithful to the council teachings must not only feel strengthened in professing that Marian devotion which has always been held with such great intensity in the Catholic Church, but must also feel drawn to model his devotion with the broad, authentic, enchanting vision which the magnificent and meaningful conciliar pages offer for the meditation and devotion of the well-provided Catholic.

The preface of these articles stresses the salvific character of the Incarnation. It uses the only Marian text from St. Paul,

"God sent his son, born of a woman" (Gal. 4:4), but this is the core of Marian formularies so important for true faith in the mystery of Christ. Jesus stands at the center of all history. He is true man because He was born of a woman, true Son of God because He had no earthly father. Thus divinity and humanity are united in the one Person of the Word so that Mary is truly the Mother of God. As we speak of the mystery of Christ we may also speak of the mystery of Mary. And as Pope Paul VI has said, "You will find Mary . . . within the whole of the Christian mystery, for devotion to her is not an end in itself, but the main road leading to Christ, to the glory of God and to love of the Church" (Sept. 12, 1963).

In the early Christian centuries the doctrine of Christ was formulated in terms of Mary. The redemptive work of Christ also can be expressed only in Marian terms. For in Mary, He came into the history of the world to deliver man from the bondage of sin and death. The Church He founded must be Marian in character, just as are His mystery and His redemptive work.

As the Mother of God, Mary bears a unique relation to each Person of the Trinity, but she is also a daughter of Adam, "redeemed in an especially sublime manner." But this exaltation does not diminish her solidarity "with all human beings in their need for salvation." This passage does not decide whether Mary is in the *debitum* of original sin, though it suggests that she is. Since she is redeemed, she is also a member of the Church, "a singular and pre-eminent member . . . and the model and excellent exemplar in faith and charity." Mary is the archetype who shows forth incomparably the nature and the position of the Church.

The divine mystery of salvation continues to be revealed to men in the Church, the Body of Christ, in which all the faithful, adhering to their Head and in fellowship with His saints, honor the memory of "Mary the ever-virgin, Mother of Jesus Christ, our Lord and God" (Canon I, Roman Mass) and ask the intercession of "blessed Mary, ever virgin" in the penitential rite at the beginning of Mass. In the Nicene Creed the Church proclaims: "For us men and for our salvation He came down from heaven: and by the power of the Holy Spirit He was born of the Virgin Mary and became man."

In their present form the Eucharistic prayers retain the thought of the ancient canon but with these variations: ". . . we honor Mary, the ever-virgin mother of Jesus Christ our Lord and God . . . born of the virgin Mary . . . Mary, the virgin Mother of God . . . in the company of the Virgin Mary, the Mother of God." An Advent preface (II) employs this phraseology: "The Virgin Mother bore him in her womb with love beyond all telling," and in a Sunday preface, "out of love for sinful man he humbled himself to be born of the Virgin."

Because Christ's work of redemption is present in the Church, we must consider His Mystical Body; we must also look at Mary's position in the Church and her relation to redeemed humanity. My principal discussion of Mary and the Church will be given in chapter 4, presenting Pope Paul's explanation of the title, as well as material from other sources.

I may note a few points of the preface to be discussed at length in later sections. One is the Annunciation, of which St. Thomas Aquinas states that Mary's fiat was spoken for the entire human race and not just for "the whole Church." I shall consider also Mary's faith, a meeting ground for ecumenical dialogue; her mediation, which is much misunderstood; her unique association with her Son in the mystery of salvation. I shall discuss the duties of redeemed mankind toward the Mother of God, a point to be developed in the chapter on Marian devotion. Mary is also the Mother of men, particularly of the faithful baptized in the name of the Trinity and made members of her Son. But in some way she is the Mother "of men" or "of all men," and not just of the faithful. Thus the Council states that its object is to describe "the position of the Blessed Virgin Mary in the mystery of the Incarnate Word and the Mystical Body, as well as the duties of the redeemed towards the Mother of God." The document is not a "complete doctrine on Mary," nor does it intend to decide those questions which have not been completely developed by theologians.

2

THE ROLE OF THE BLESSED VIRGIN IN THE ECONOMY OF SALVATION (55-59)

55. The sacred Scriptures of both the Old and the New Testament, as well as ancient tradition, show the role of the Mother of the Savior in the economy of salvation in an ever clearer light and propose it as something to be probed into. The books of the Old Testament recount the period of salvation history during which the coming of Christ into the world was slowly prepared for. These earliest documents, as they are read in the Church and are understood in the light of a further and full revelation, bring the figure of the woman, Mother of the Redeemer, into a gradually sharper focus.

When looked at in this way, she is already prophetically foreshadowed in that victory over the serpent which was promised to our first parents after their fall into sin [cf. Gen. 3:15]. Likewise she is the virgin who is to conceive and bear a son, whose name will be called Emmanuel [cf. Isa. 7:14; Mic. 5:2-3; Matt. 1:22-23]. She stands out among the poor and humble of the Lord, who confidently await and receive salvation from Him. With her, the exalted Daughter of Sion, and after a long expectation of the promise, the times were at length fulfilled and the new dispensation established. All this occurred when the Son of God took a human nature from her, that He might in the mysteries of His flesh free man from sin.

56. The Father of mercies willed that the consent of the predestined mother should precede the Incarnation, so that just as a woman contributed to death, so also a woman should contribute to life. This contrast was verified in outstanding fashion by the Mother of Jesus. She gave to the world that very Life which renews all things, and she was enriched by God with gifts befitting such a role.

It is no wonder, then, that the usage prevailed among the holy Fathers whereby they called the Mother of God entirely holy and free from all stain of sin, fashioned by the Holy Spirit into a kind of new substance and new creature.[1] Adorned from the first instant of her conception with the splendors of an entirely unique holiness, the Virgin of Nazareth is, on God's command, greeted by an angel messenger as "full of grace" [cf. Luke 1:28]. To the heavenly messenger she replies: "Behold the handmaid of the Lord; be it done to me according to thy word" [Luke 1:38].

By thus consenting to the divine utterance, Mary, a daughter of Adam, became the Mother of Jesus. Embracing God's saving will with a full heart and impeded by no sin, she devoted herself totally as a handmaid of the Lord to the person and work of her Son. In subordination to Him and along with Him, by the grace of almighty God she served the mystery of redemption.

Rightly therefore the holy Fathers see her as used by God not merely in a passive way, but as cooperating in the work of human salvation through free faith and obedience. For, as St. Irenaeus says, she, "being obedient, became the cause of salvation for herself and for the whole human race."[2] Hence in their preaching not a few of the early Fathers gladly assert with him: "The knot of Eve's disobedience was untied by Mary's obedience. What the Virgin Eve bound through her unbelief, Mary loosened by her faith."[3] Comparing Mary with Eve, they call her "the mother of the living,"[4] and still more often they say: "death through Eve, life through Mary."[5]

57. This union of the Mother with the Son in the work of salvation was manifested from the time of Christ's virginal conception up to His death. It is shown first of all when Mary, arising

---

[1] Cf. Germanus of Constantinople, *Hom. in Annunt. Deiparae:* PG 98, 328 A, and his *Hom. in Dorm.,* 2: PG 98, 357; St. Anastasius of Antioch, *Serm. 2 de Annunt.,* 2: PG 89, 1377AB, and his *Serm. 3 de Annunt.,* 2 PG 89, 1388C; St. Andrew of Crete, *Can. in B.V. Nat.,* 4: PG 97, 1321B, and his *In B.V. Nat.,* I: PG 97, 812A, as well as his *Hom. in Dorm.,* PG 97, 1068C; and St. Sophronius *Or. 2 in Annunt.* 18: PG 87 (3), 3237BD.

[2] St. Irenaeus, *Adv. Haer.,* III, 22, 4: PG 7, 959 *Adv. Haer.* 2, 123.

[3] *Ibid.,* 2, 124.

[4] St. Epiphanius, *Haer.,* 78, 18: PG 42, 728 CD-729AB.

[5] St. Jerome, *Epist.,* 22, 21: PL 22, 408CF., St. Augustine, *Serm.,* 51, 2, 3: PL 38, 335, and his *Serm.,* 232, PL 38, 1108; St. Cyril of Jerusalem, *Catech.,* 12, 15: PG 33, 741AB; St. John Chrysostom, *In Ps.,* 44, 7: PG 55, 193; and St. John of Damascus, *Hom. 2 in Dorm. B.V.M.,* 3: PG 96 728.

in haste to go to visit Elizabeth, was greeted by her as blessed because of her belief in the promise of salvation, while the precursor leaped with joy in the womb of his mother [cf. Luke 1:41-45]. This association was shown also at the birth of our Lord, who did not diminish His mother's virginal integrity but sanctified it,[6] when the Mother of God joyfully showed her first-born Son to the shepherds and Magi.

When she presented Him to the Lord in the temple, making the offering of the poor, she heard Simeon foretelling at the same time that her Son would be a sign of contradiction and that a sword would pierce the mother's soul, that out of many hearts thoughts might be revealed [cf. Luke 2:34-35]. When the Child Jesus was lost and they had sought Him sorrowing, His parents found Him in the temple, taken up with the things which were His father's business. They did not understand the reply of the Son. But His Mother, to be sure, kept all these things to be pondered over in her heart [cf. Luke 2:41-51].

58. In the public life of Jesus, Mary made significant appearances. This was so even at the very beginning, when she was moved by pity at the marriage feast of Cana, and her intercession brought about the beginning of miracles by Jesus the Messiah [cf. John 2:11]. In the course of her Son's preaching she received His praise when, in extolling a kingdom beyond the calculations and bonds of flesh and blood, He declared blessed [cf. Mark 3:35; Luke 11:27-28] those who heard and kept the Word of God, as she was faithfully doing [cf. Luke 2:19, 51].

Thus the Blessed Virgin advanced in her pilgrimage of faith, and loyally preserved in her union with her Son unto the cross. There she stood, in keeping with the divine plan [cf. John 19:25], suffering grievously with her only-begotten Son. There she united herself with a maternal heart to His sacrifice, and lovingly consented to the immolation of this Victim which she herself had brought forth. Finally, the same Christ Jesus dying on the cross gave her as a mother to His disciple. This He did when He said: "Woman, behold thy son" [John 19:26-27].[7]

59. But since it pleased God not to manifest solemnly the mystery of the salvation of the human race until He poured forth the Spirit promised by Christ, we see the apostles before the day

---

[6] Cf. *Lateran Council of the year 649, can.* 3: *Mansi,* 10, 1151; St. Leo the Great, *Epist. ad Flav.,* PL 54, 759; *Council of Chalcedon: Mansi,* 7, 462; and St. Ambrose, *De inst. virg.,* PL 16, 320.

[7] Cf. Pius XII, encyclical *Mystici Corporis,* June 29, 1943: *AAS,* 35 (1943), pp. 247-48.

of Pentecost "continuing with one mind in prayer with the women and Mary, the Mother of Jesus, and with His brethren" [Acts 1:14]. We see Mary prayerfully imploring the gift of the Spirit, who had already overshadowed her in the Annunciation.

Finally, preserved free from all guilt of original sin,[8] the immaculate Virgin was taken up body and soul into heavenly glory upon the completion of her earthly sojourn.[9] She was exalted by the Lord as Queen of all, in order that she might be the more thoroughly conformed to her Son, the Lord of lords (cf. Apoc. 19:16) and the conqueror of sin and death.[10]

This second section considers Mary's role in the mystery of salvation and so in the life and activity of our Redeemer.

There is a twofold evolution in the history of salvation: the People of God prepare for the event of the Word made flesh, and they grow in faith as the revelation unfolds before them. In the divine plan creation and the history of God's people were always ordained to the incarnation of the Word. Pre-Christian salvation history prepared for that central event of all history in which Mary had an essential role. In the preparation for the coming of Christ the figure of Mary emerges. "These earliest documents, as they are read in the Church and are understood in the light of a further and full revelation, bring the figure of the woman, Mother of the Redeemer, into a gradually sharper focus." Holy Scripture is not a document complete in itself without laws of interpretation. It has grown out of the People of God and can be understood only in the light of faith. The Holy Spirit animates the Church and is needed for the proper understanding of what the sacred books say.

---

[8] Cf. Pius IX, bull *Ineffabilis,* Dec. 8, 1854: *Acta Pii IX,* 1, I, p. 616; Den. 1641 (2803).

[9] Cf. Pius XII, apostolic constitution *Munificentissimus,* Nov. 1, 1950: *AAS* 42 (1950), p. 770 (*Denz.* 2333 3903) Cf. St. John of Damascus, *Enc. in dorm. Dei genitricis, Hom. 1 and 3*: PG 96, 721-61, especially 728B; St. Germanus of Constantinople, *In S. gen. dorm., Serm. 1*: PG 98 (6), 340-48 as well as his *Serm. 3*: PG 86 (2), 3277-3312.

[10] Cf. Pius XII, encyclical *Ad Caeli Reginam,* Oct. 11, 1954: *AAS* 46 (1954), pp. 633-36 (*Denz.* 3913 ff.). Cf. St. John of Damascus, *De fide Orth.,* IV, 14: PG 94, 1153-61, and St. Andrew of Crete, *Hom. 3 in dorm. SS. Deiparae*: PG 97, 1089-1109.

The authors of the Marian chapter purposely avoid the use of the term "co-redemptrix," for while it admits of a correct interpretation, it is also susceptible of grave misunderstanding. They also tread lightly on such controversial ground as the famous promise of the proto-gospel (Gen. 3:15) that Adam's seed shall bruise the serpent's head, because of an erroneous translation in the Vulgate (*"she* shall bruise your head," instead of *it*—that is, the seed, referring either to man in general or to the Messiah). The Constitution *Ineffabilis Deus* of 1854 defining the Immaculate Conception had still taken this as a proof passage referring to Mary's own victory over the serpent. The present document is content to say that Mary is "prophetically foreshadowed in the promise of victory over the serpent," with a modest "cf. Gen. 3:15" in parentheses. After further reference to the familiar Isaiah prophecy of the virgin who is to bear a son, the chapter sees in her the daughter of Sion in a special way, as she appears in the early chapters of Luke's Gospel a concept stressed by Stanislaus Lyonnet, S.J., and René Laurentin and others. Mary is the type of the poor and humble who long for salvation; she brings the expectant People of God into the age of fulfillment when the Incarnation of the Word answers the longing of mankind for salvation.

It was the Father's will that Mary should accept the Incarnation before it came about. And He prepared her by His gifts for her great office. This is the teaching of the fathers of the Church, who "call the Mother of God all-holy and free of every stain of sin, as though fashioned and formed by the Holy Spirit into a new creature." They saw this fullness of meaning in the angel's greeting to Mary at the Annunciation: "Hail, full of grace" (or "favored one"). Mary's answer to the angel, "Behold, I am the handmaid of the Lord; let it be to me according to your word" (Luke 1:38), shows that as the Lord's humble handmaid she dedicated herself to the person and work of her Son.

Encouragement toward unity through love and study of the Blessed Virgin is shown in various writings today. For example, in an article in the *United Church Herald* at Christmas in 1966, Dr. Roger Hazelton of Andover—Newton Theological School, near Boston, asked for a re-evaluation by Protestants of Mary's role in the mystery of the Incarnation. He said—

> Protestants generally have been unwilling to grant her as large a share as the gospel of Luke suggests. The place of Mary in our faith must always be determined by her relationship to Jesus Christ . . . Mary represents humanity standing on tip-toe to receive and follow Christ . . . We do her no true honor by separating her from the mass of mankind whose representative she is from the cradle to the cross. For Mary does not stand alone; her place is from first to last beside the Son of God. Her true greatness is to be found . . . in her closeness—her close and incomparable relationship to the "great things" God had done for her and for us all. All that greatness is enhanced by Mary's own acceptance of her closeness, her humble and obedient rejoicing in the Lord.

Jesus existed *before* His mother. He is the only son who was in a position to *choose* His mother. He could choose, therefore, what every son would choose if he could, the mother who would suit him best. Further, it is of the very heart of sonship that a son wants to give his mother gifts; and Christ, being God, could give her all that she might desire; to His giving power there was no limit. And what above all she wanted was union with God, the most complete union possible to a human being of her will with God's will, grace therefore in her soul.

Jesus was her Son, and He gave His love lavishly. Mary responded totally, so that she was sinless. It was her response to the grace of God that made her supreme in holiness—higher even than the highest angel. We may pause for a moment to look at this truth. By nature Mary was lower than the least angel for human nature as such is less than angelic. But any relation in the order of grace is higher than any in the order of nature. It is through grace that we become closer to God— by our response, that is, to the created share in His own life that God offers us. Through grace the Virgin Mary outranks all created beings, but only because she responded more perfectly. As St. John Chrysostom says: "She would not have been blessed, though she had borne Him in the body, had she not heard the Word of God and kept it."

In the New Testament we find the dispositions of Mary presented by Luke with obvious deliberation. We see the act of obedience by which Mary made good the fall of the first woman, "so that just as a woman contributed to death, so also a woman should contribute to life." Mary gave "that very life which renews all things."

This contrast between Mary and Eve was a favorite thought of the fathers of the Church, as we shall note later. From the earliest times tradition has completed the parallel between Adam and Christ (Rom. 5:12-19; I Cor. 15:22) with the parallel between Eve and Mary. Indeed, Mary is less correlative with the Second Adam than Eve is with the First Adam. But the decision of faith by which she conceived the life that renews the world is not a casual assent of just another person; it enters as a true cause into the salvation of all men. With her response to the angel she stands at the head of all mankind in receiving salvation, summing up the assent of faith. Mary is part of humanity and is intimately associated with the divine plan of salvation. But she is not so close to Christ as to derogate from His unique character as Saviour. In faith she received the mission and the message of the Redeemer, and she conceived Him in her heart and in her body. She did so by the grace of the coming Redeemer, as His handmaid "devoted . . . totally to the Person and work of her Son."

We speak of the centrality of Christ, and we must. But at the same time we must be mindful of the place of Mary together with Him: "In subordination to Him and along with Him, by the grace of almighty God she served the mystery of redemption." Mary, mother of the Redeemer, is the dominant theme of this section. Mary exists because of Christ; she has meaning only because of Him. She cooperated in the work of "human salvation through free faith and obedience." She "consented to the immolation of the victim she had brought forth."

Within the context of the Mary-Eve relation emerges the

association of Jesus and Mary, so necessary for an understanding of her role in salvation history and of the Catholic emphasis on Mary's role in the Church. The fathers have spoken of one man and one woman—Adam and Eve, Christ and Mary; later writers like to speak of the inseparability of Jesus and Mary in the mystery of man's salvation and sanctification. This is important for an understanding of the relation of Son and Mother in salvation history as well as for understanding her role in His entire incarnate life. We note these phrases: "the union of the Mother with the Son"—"persevered with her Son unto the cross"—"she united herself with a maternal heart to his sacrifice"—and finally in glory she "is conformed to her Son."

Mary is inseparable from her Son, and her role and function are completely united to His. Her glory rests upon Him; her holiness is derived from Him.

> Who can estimate the holiness and perfection of her who was chosen to be the Mother of Christ? [Newman asks in one of the Oxford sermons (Mar. 25, 1832).] If to him that hath, more is given, and holiness and divine favour go together (and this we are expressly told) what must have been the transcendent purity of her whom the Creator Spirit condescended to overshadow with His miraculous presence? What must have been her gifts, who was chosen to be the only near earthly relative of the Son of God, the only one whom He was bound by nature to revere and look up to; the one appointed to train and educate Him, to instruct Him day by day, as He grew in wisdom and stature? This contemplation runs to a high subject, did we dare to follow it; for what, think you, was the sanctified state of that human nature of which God formed His sinless Son; knowing, as we do that "that which is born of the flesh." Nothing is so calculated to impress on our minds that Christ is really partaker of our nature, and in all respects man, save sin only, as to associate Him with the thought of her, by ministration He became our Brother.
>
> There is no part of the history of Jesus but Mary has her part in it. There are those who profess to be His servants, who think that her work was ended when she bore Him and after that she had nothing to do and be forgotten . . . She brought the tender infant into the temple, she lifted Him up in her arms when the wise men came to adore Him. She fled with Him to Egypt, she took Him

to Jerusalem when He was twelve years old. He lived with her at Nazarath for thirty years. She was with Him at the marriage feast. Even when He had left her to preach, she hovered about Him and shows herself as He toils along the sacred way with the cross on His shoulders.

I shall develop both ideas at greater length, but first I should like to refer to some other ideas less emphasized but important for an understanding of the theology of Mary.

In the phrase "predestined mother" some commentators might find an implicit reference to the thought of St. Bernardine of Siena and other Franciscans. They taught that not only was the Incarnation willed from all eternity apart from the fall of Adam (according to the thought of John Duns Scotus, William of Ware, and St. Lawrence of Brindisi) but Mary was predestined also to be the mother of the Incarnate Word. This concept does not seem to be contained, at least explicitly, in the words of the Constitution.

Here we devote some thought to the parallel of Eve and Mary. The document refers to the statement of St. Irenaeus (d. 202) early in Christian tradition, the first part of the third century: "As Eve who had Adam as her husband but was nevertheless a virgin, was disobedient, and thereby became the cause of death to herself and to the whole of mankind, so also Mary was, had a pre-ordained husband and was still a virgin, by her obedience became a cause of her own salvation and the salvation of the whole human race" (*Against Heresies,* 3:22). The phrase "cause of salvation" is probably the most important title for Mary in the context of this passage, and the Eve-Mary analogy favored by Irenaeus has been applied by theologians and spiritual writers ever since. He also stated: ". . . the knot of Eve's disobedience had its untying by means of Mary's obedience; what Eve the virgin tied by her unbelief the Virgin Mary untied by faith." Various fathers, notably St. Justin, St. Augustine, and St. Ambrose, compare Mary with Eve and call her "the true mother of the living." Their thought may be tersely stated in the phrase "Death through Eve, life through Mary."

St. Augustine put it this way—

By a woman came death and by a woman came life; by Eve destruction, by Mary salvation. The former was corrupted and followed the deceiver; the latter remaining inviolate, gave birth to the savior. The former willingly accepted the draught proffered by the serpent and gave it to her husband whence came the penalty of death; the latter by an infusion of heavenly grace from above brought forth the Life who is able to quicken even the flesh of the dead. Who is the author of this but He who is the Son of a Virgin and the Spouse of Virgins, He who brought His Mother fecundity without destroying her virginity.

St. Leo the Great (440–461), who served as pope during the Augustine's century (d. 430), speaks of the "mystery of reconciliation" being fulfilled by a man and a woman as an antithesis of Adam and Eve—

The mystery of our reconciliation ordained from all eternity was not fulfilled by any figures. For the Holy Spirit had not yet come upon the Virgin nor had the power of the Most High overshadowed her, that Wisdom building herself a house in a virginal womb, the Word might become flesh and the form of God and the form of a servant being united in one person, the Creator of all time might be born in time, and He by whom all things were made might Himself be conceived among all those things. For unless the new man, made in the likeness of sinful flesh, had taken our old man, and He who is consubstantial with the Father had deigned also to be consubstantial with His Mother, and He who is alone free from sin had united our nature to Himself, all mankind would have remained captive under the yoke of the devil.

St. Bernard of Clairvaux, an illustrious Marion doctor, says—

One man and one woman, dearly beloved, have harmed us; but nonetheless, thanks be to God, by one man and one woman, all is restored to us and with great increase of grace. The gift is not in proportion to the offense; for the magnitude of the benefit exceeds the measure of the injury. So, to be sure, the most wise and merciful creator did not entirely shatter that which was broken but remade it entirely in a better way: in that he formed an Adam for us out of the old and transformed Eve into Mary.

Cardinal Newman commented on the Mary-Eve parallel in his *Essay on Development*—

Certainly the parallel between the "mother of all living" and the Mother of the Redeemer may be gathered from a comparison of the first chapters of scripture with the last. It was noticed in a former place that the only passage where the serpent is directly identified with the evil spirit occurs in the twentieth chapter of Revelations; now it is observable that the recognition when made, is found in the course of a vision of a "woman clothed with the sun, and the moon under her feet." Thus two women are brought into contrast with each other. Moreover, as it is said in the Apocalypse, "the dragon was wrought with the woman and went to make war with the remnant of her seed," so it is prophesied in Genesis, "I will put enmity between thee and the woman and between they seed and her seed. He shall bruise thy head and thou shalt bruise his heel." Also the enmity was to exist not only between the serpent and the seed of the woman, but between the serpent and the woman herself; and here too there is a correspondence in the Apocalyptic vision. If then there is reason for thinking that this mystery at the close of the scripture record answer to the mystery in the beginning of it and that "the Woman" mentioned in both passages is one and the same then she can be none other than S. Mary, thus introduced prophetically to our notice immediately on the transgression of Eve.

In a letter to Dr. Pusey, Newman makes this point about the image of the Woman—

I do not deny that under the image of the Woman, the Church is signified; but what I would maintain is this, that the holy Apostle would not have spoken of the Church under this particular image *unless* there had existed a Blessed Virgin Mary, who was exalted on high and the object of veneration to all the faithful."

For him the Apocalypse gives special treatment to Our Lady—

It is sometimes asked, Why do not the sacred writers mention our Lady's greatness? I answer she was or may have been alive when the apostles and evangelists wrote;—there was just one book of scripture certainly written after her death and that book does (if I may so speak) canonise her." [Ibid.]

Our Lady appears in a significant way at the starting point
of Jesus' public life. As related by St. John (2:1-11), at the
marriage feast of Cana she noticed the distress of the young
bride and bridegroom when the wine failed. Commentators
discuss whether or not she was asking her Son for a miracle,
and the meaning of His reply: "O woman, what have you to
do with me? My hour has not yet come." This seems a declaration of independence, but Jesus adds that when the hour of
His suffering and glorification (which is what "hour" means
in St. John) has come, it will be different. The Constitution,
however, will not decide these disputed matters, but rather
goes to the heart of the event: ". . . she was moved by pity
. . . and at her intercession brought about the beginning of
the miracles by Jesus the Messiah." For Mary, knowing that
He would not refuse to do something, said to the servants,
"Do whatever he tells you." And so the changing of water into
wine, His inaugural miracle, is done at His mother's asking,
"and his disciples believed in him."

Vincent McNabb, O.P., famous English Dominican writer
and preacher of a past generation, has a lovely appreciation
of the marriage feast of Cana. In his *Meditations on the
Gospel of St. John* he writes—

And here is this exquisitely beautiful scene of Our Lady present at
a wedding feast. There is something special about it that needs to
be remembered in this age of decaying home life. The Mother of
Jesus was there—and Jesus and His disciples were invited. I can
quite imagine Our Lady saying "if you invite me you will have to
invite my Son." And He would say, "if you invite me the Twelve
will have to come too." (I have often wondered if that accounted
for the shortage of wine—having to provide for twelve extra guests
would strain any wine-cellar.)

It is so delightful that when there was a wedding feast in that
place Our Lady was there. (It is not worth-while having a wedding
unless you have Our Lady there.) And she may have said, "I have
come only on one condition—that I am in the kitchen." Of course
on a wedding day at least one person has to keep her head; so
Our Lady said, "I will be in the kitchen." They said, "You will
see that everything goes right?" And she said she would, and, as
we know, she did. When the wine ran short she went to her Son

and said: "They have no wine." That just lifts a little bit of the veil and shows us the relationship of human mother to a divine Son. Like that bit that was moved when St. Luke describes how Our Lady and St. Joseph find the Boy—the almost run-away Boy—and Our Lady says, "Thy father and I have sought Thee sorrowing."

They had been weeping for Him. That was all—but quite enough. He went back with them for eighteen years. Nothing for Himself—*they* are sorrowing. What a perfect principle that is— eighteen years ago she had said, "We are sorrowing." He had His Father's work to do and His Mother's will. And at the end of that time I can hear her saying, "No, my dear child, you must leave me. You must go to them. You are theirs. They are sorrowing." It is Our Lady's way of giving to the Incarnate Son his obedience to work. "They have no wine." She took from her own lips the goblet of wine that was Jesus himself. This scene is of unparalleled tenderness; that tenderness which is close to both laughter and tears. I am never quite certain of myself when I preach about this —I never know whether I shall break down. The love in it is so exquisite—that Mother's love, that child's love, the love of the Mother for that Son, the love of that Son for the Mother, the love of both for me! We can think about it and if God allowed us, for instance, to dream about it tonight, what dreams would be ours. We ought to meditate again and again on the marriage feast of Cana.

Some Catholic and Anglican commentators see in the verses (especially as St. John continues "Jesus knowing that all was now fulfilled") a fulfillment of Genesis 3:15. The enmity between the woman and her seed (Christ) and the serpent (the Devil) and his seed (John 8:44) culminates in the victory of Christ, the Second Adam, on the cross (John 12:31-32) while His mother, the Second Eve, stands beside Him. They also think that more is involved in Jesus' words to His mother and His disciple than a request to look after her, for in Genesis 3:20 Eve is called "the mother of all the living," and Mary's is a universal spiritual motherhood. Some authors point out the great importance that seems to be attached to the text, that it is not the disciple but Mary who is addressed first and that the woman in the twelfth chapter of the Apocalypse, with her seed, the Christians, seems to be a figure not only of the Church but also of Mary. If this is correct, there

is a scriptural basis for what the Church has come to understand: Jesus has given us all to Mary as her sons, and her to
us as our mother. But the Council, faithful to its determination not to settle such matters but to leave them to be worked
out, makes no mention of all this. It simply declares that Mary
loyally maintained her union with her Son at the cross; that
it was by the divine plan that she stood there; she grieved
bitterly with her only child and joined with a mother's heart
in His sacrifice by giving a loving consent to the offering of
the victim who had taken birth from her. At the end, when
Jesus was dying on the cross, He gave her as mother to His
disciple with these words: "Woman, behold your son" (John
19.26).

The spirit of Mary's faith carried through all the events
that combine her life with the Lord's. There are samples from
the New Testament—the Visitation, the birth of Jesus, the
coming of the Magi, the Presentation in the Temple. Mary did
not fully understand all these events but kept them to be
pondered in her heart. Then came Cana, the public life of
Jesus, and Calvary. Mary lived by faith—in the life, work, and
sufferings of her Son— and the meaning of this faith is for the
rest of men. While Mary shares in the mission of Jesus, it is
not all completely clear to her. Because of her unwavering faith
she is the model of the community of those who hear the
word of God and keep it. Redeemed mankind also lives by
faith and love and shares in the redemptive mission of Christ,
though not to be compared with Mary.

At the present time the Church seems to be giving new
emphasis to the faith of Our Lady. We find this point emphasized by St. Bernard in his famous sermon "The Twelve
Stars," used in the office for the feast of the Sorrows of Our
Lady for September 15. In the final part of the quotation he
speaks of Mary's faith—

> The martyrdom of the Virgin is set before us both in the prophecy
> of Simeon and in the story of the Lord's passion. The saintly old
> man had said of the child Jesus "Behold this Child is destined for
> a sign which shall be contradicted." To Mary he said: "And your

own soul a sword shall pierce." Yes, truly O Blessed Mother, the sword pierced your soul. Only by passing through your soul could it penetrate to the body of your Son. When Jesus your Son had given up His spirit, when the cruel spear which pierced His side could no longer touch His soul, it transfixed yours. His soul was no longer there, but your was; it could not be torn away.

The sword of sorrow did indeed pierce your soul. We call you more than martyr because of your love, which made you suffer with your Son, brought pain of soul far more exquisite than any pain of body. "Woman behold your son." Was not this word of your Son far more piercing than any sword as it thrust in and cut apart soul and spirit? O what an exchange! You were given John for Jesus, the servant for the Lord, the disciple for the Master, the Son of Zebedee for the Son of God, mere man for very God. How keenly those words must have pierced your loving soul! The mere remembrance of them can wring with sorrow our steely hearts.

Do not wonder that Mary is said to be martyred in spirit. He only may wonder who has forgotten the words of the Apostle Paul. When he wrote of the sins of the gentiles he placed among their greatest ones that they were without affection. Such want of affection was far from Mary's heart. May it be equally far from those of her servants!

Some people may comment, "But she must have known beforehand that He was going to die." Yes, she knew it. "Had she no hope that He would rise again?' Yes, she had hope; *she had absolute faith.* "Did she, in spite of this, mourn for her crucified Son?" Yes, and deeply. Do you marvel less that the Son of Mary suffered than that Mary suffered with Him? He could die in body. Could she not have died with Him in her heart? His death was brought about by a love greater than any man has; hers by a love no other creature ever had except she. [Sermon "The Twelve Stars"]

Cardinal Newman discusses the sorrows of Mary in this way—

It is expressly noted of her that she stood by the cross. She did not grovel in the dust, but stood upright to blows, to stabs, which the long passion of her Son inflicted upon her every moment.

But He who bore the sinners [shame for sinners] spared His Mother who was sinless this supreme indignity. Not in the body but in the soul she suffered. True, in His agony she was agonized; in His passion she suffered a fellow-passion; she was crucified with Him; the spear that pierced His breast pierced through her spirit.

Yet there were not visible signs of this intimate martyrdom; she stood up, still collected, motionless, solitary, under the cross of her Son, surrounded by angels, and shrouded in her virginal sanctity from the notice of all who were taking part in His crucifixion.

Pope John XXIII also comments on Mary's composure at the foot of the cross—

> Life and death are the two significant and decisive elements of Christ's sacrifice. From His smile at Bethlehem the same smile which lights up the faces of all the children of men when they first appear on earth, to His last gasp and sob on the cross, which gathered all our sufferings into one to hallow them, and wiped away all our sins by atoning for them we have seen how Christ lived in this our earthly life. And Mary is still there, beside the cross, as she was beside the Babe of Bethlehem. Let us pray to her, this Mother, pray to her so that she too may pray for us "now and at the hour of our death."

After He had preached for three years the day came when His own mother accompanied Him to Calvary and stood at the foot of the cross. Her Son was crucified; He gave His life for all men. Mary did not give way to terrible and incomparable grief. She knew that now His real triumph was to begin, so with motherly love she obeyed the last request of her dying Son when He entrusted us all, in the person of the Apostle John, to her care. So, through the sacrifice of Christ and around His cross we have all become sons by adoption of His most holy Mother and we may call ourselves brothers of Jesus.

"Standing by the cross of Jesus was his mother. . . . When Jesus saw his mother, and the disciple whom he loved standing near, he said to his mother, 'Woman, behold your son!' Then He said to the disciple, 'Behold your mother!' And from that hour the disciple took her to his own home." [John 19: 25-27.] St. John links Cana and this passage in his own manner by a repetition of three words: "Mother . . . woman . . . hour." It is one of the five scenes he mentions on Calvary: the title on the cross proclaming Jesus King (Messiah), the parting of his garments by the soldiers; their casting lots on his tunic; "I thirst"; and the piercing of his side, no bone being broken. The last converges on Calvary, and the other four scenes are clear fulfillments of prophecy.

Christian art and devotion are fond of depicting the sorrows of Mary at the cross of her Son. Writers too have sought to capture the feelings of Mary as she took part in the suffering and death of her beloved Son. A contemporary writer, Father Josef Weiger, has thus depicted the Sorrowful Mother, the *Pieta*—

> She stood under the dry tree of her Son's ignominy and this tree was henceforth through all ages to be a prophetic and eternally valid sign, the most venerated, the most feared. She was utterly given up to the will of God, suffering with Christ, giving back to God the Son of God, crucified with Him as her immolation and herself as fellow victim; God appointed deacon at the sacrifice of redemption; representative of the Church-to-be. To her greater torment, Mary must read on the inscription over Jesus's head the word Nazareth; and the bliss and the mystery of that quiet home where she and Jesus lived so long together flashed into her troubled soul.
>
> "Thus bitter death doth part"; and once more Mary held her Child upon her lap, her arms around Him, covering His brow with her kisses, with streaming tears beholding the searing marks . . . inflicted on His most sacred face. Again and again throughout Christian times artists have tried their hand at depicting this scene; Mary with her Son's dead body. So Jesus' life ended as it had begun in Bethlehem, in His mother's arms. . . . [*Mary, Mother of Our Faith*]

Here we may further comment on the faith of Mary. The document states that "the Blessed Virgin advanced in her pilgrimage of faith" and it also speaks of her faith in other contexts. "What the virgin Eve bound through her unbelief, Mary loosened by her faith" (St. Irenaeus). She heard and kept the Word of God "as she was faithfully doing" (cf. Lk. 2:19,51), in a pre-eminent way beyond that of the holiest person or the most zealous disciple. Her life of faith makes her like other members of the Church; it was spent in the darkness of faith and not in light as some

would ascribe practical omniscience to her even in the first
moment of her conception.

But Mary lived by faith at the time of the Incarnation, at
the birth of Christ, the visit of the Magi, and those happy and
mysterious days at Nazareth. Brother Max Thurian of Taize,
France, phrases it in this way—

> The Gospel tells us that "the Child grew and increased in wisdom"
> and that "the grace of God rested upon him" (Luke 2:40). This
> reference reveals at one and at the same time the reality of the
> divine nature in Jesus and also the discreet manner of its appear-
> ance. Was it not also said of John the Baptist with practically the
> same words "the child grew and increased in spirit" (Luke 1:50)?
> In the course of this first period of Christ's childhood, Mary lived
> by faith in the promises of God from the time of conception and
> birth of Jesus, and not in the permanent company of an infant
> prodigy who was forever revealing Himself as God. But this faith
> was "the assurance of things hoped for, the certainty of things not
> seen" (Heb. 11:1). Without the miraculous sign which had
> marked the conception and birth of Christ, while yet keeping and
> meditating on them in her heart, Mary lived in the faith that one
> day there would be revealed the Messiah of whom she knew her-
> self to be the Mother.
>
> If Jesus had constantly been revealed in His divine nature dur-
> ing His childhood, Mary would have had no need of faith nor
> would she have been surprised at the reply of her Son at the age
> of twelve: "Why did you seek me? Did you not know that I must
> be about My Father's business?" (Luke 2:49.) She knows that He
> is the Son of God, but she also knows that she must live in the
> hope of faith, until He enters upon His supernatural mission as
> the Messiah. When He is twelve it seems to her that she must
> still be His cautious mother and that the humanity of the Son of
> God still demands her quite human mothering. She does not seek
> to hasten the time of fulfillment as she will at Cana. She remains
> always the happy believer, she who lives above all by faith. Mary
> also, as a human creature, is saved by faith and not by sight. As
> Luther wrote of her: "She not only has the glory of being Mother
> and Virgin, of being the Mother of the Son of God, but she has
> also eternal salvation by faith; she does not obtain this salvation
> because she is Mother and Virgin, Mother of the Son of God. It
> was always possible for her to fall but she is the eternal dwelling-
> place of the Holy Spirit and she remains perpetually holy, and
> blessed Mother for eternity."

God chose Abraham without giving him any special reason why. By virtue of this covenant God called the patriarch to faith and to the consequences of this faith: separation from the heathen setting and trustful obedience to the divine will. The liturgy honors Abraham as "father of our faith."

The election of Abraham concerned not only his person and his posterity but all the nations of the world (Gen. 12:3). His name was changed from Abram to Abraham, "father of the peoples" (Gen. 17:5), and through him all the nations were to share in salvation.

Abraham's faith was the pivot on which the entire history of Israel was based. The role of this people in the plan of salvation and their very existence depended on the acceptance of the divine invitation given to Abraham beside his tent in the oak trees of Mambre. But his act of faith was almost nothing compared with the faith of Mary, to whom the angel promised: "You shall conceive in your womb and you shall bear a son" (Luke 1:31). The blessing of God for Israel depended on the depth of its faith, and the grace for the human race depended on the fiat of the Virgin Mary, Mother of God and mother of all men.

Abraham's faith was that of Israel. He was not just a man on whom the fate of Israel depended. He was Israel as it existed, the beginning of that race. His faith was the response of Israel to its God and would remain as the bond uniting the People of God and giving supernatural continuity with Abraham, "the father of all the faithful" (Rom. 4:11). Mary's faith was that of the Church; she sums up and personifies in herself the entire Church. In the divine-human transaction which took place in Nazareth she replies with full consent: "Be it done unto me."

Mary's faith was the supreme act elicited in the Church, for while the brief message of the angel left many details hidden, the development would be further specified in the revelation to which she adhered totally with a firmness and purity never to be equaled by any believer in her Son.

The faith of Abraham preceded the actual covenant be-

tween God and himself and prepared for it. This was only
natural; it was precisely the disposition necessary to receive
the promise on which the covenant was based, since the promised blessings came from a free act of God's infinite love and
surpassed natural expectations. Abraham's faith began as far
back as his departure from his native country, from obedience
to God (Gen. 12:1). The covenant announced and entered
into did not receive its solemn ratification until later, in the
blood of the circumcision (Gen. 17).

So also the new covenant solemnized in the blood of the
Saviour on the altar of the cross was prepared for and entered
into by virtue of Mary's faith at the time of the Annunciation.
Mary is a principle in the entire order of Redemption and
Atonement and not merely of that part which follows her in
time—just as Jesus was the Redeemer in His humanity for
those under the Old Law as well as those of the New. The
graces dispensed in the Old Dispensation were due to the
Saviour's redemptive work, and in this work Mary's faith had
a part. The just persons of the Old Law are principles in the
whole redemptive order, though in different ways. If Abraham
is her father according to the flesh, she is his mother in the
order of grace.

In Israel the promise would remain the principal matter
of faith, though gradually it became more and more precisely
defined, qualified, and spiritualized in the course of history. In
the Church the principal matter of faith is not the promise but
the inner mysteries of God. Still these mysteries are revealed
to Mary only indirectly in the announcement of the good news
of salvation, which is in the form of a promise; and if the
mysteries are revealed at all, it is only because it is in them
that the promised beatitude will be attained. In the Church,
as in Israel, faith is of such a nature as to engender hope, and
the "congregation of the faithful" perpetuates the type of faith
initially elicited in Mary.

To both Abraham and Mary a son was promised: to Abraham is spite of his advanced age and his wife's sterility; to
Mary in spite of the virginity she was to preserve. In both in-

stances the offspring would be "great" (Gen. 13:16, 15:5; Luke 1:32). Abraham was told that kings would come forth from him (Gen. 17:6); Mary, that her son "would be given the throne of David his father" and that he would be "king over the house of Jacob" (Luke 1:32). Abraham's posterity would receive "the land of Canaan as an everlasting possession" (Gen. 17:8); the kingdom of Mary's son would be endless (Luke 1:32). Abraham would be a "blessing" to all the families of the earth (Gen. 12:2,3); all generations would call Mary blessed (Luke 1:48). Abraham was forewarned that suffering awaited his son; they would be "strangers in a land not their own; they would be slaves there and oppressed for four hundred years (Gen. 15:13). Mary was told by Simeon that her son would be "a sign that shall be contradicted."

To prepare for his role Abraham was required to leave his country, his kindred, and his father's house and enter the land which the Lord was to show him (Gen. 12:1) A parallel for Mary can be seen in the tradition of her presentation in the Temple. It is above all in a spiritual sense that Mary was obliged to leave her father's house and her own country by entering into a supernatural order in which human nature was a "stranger." Mary's spiritual motherhood embraced all men.

This separation is most obvious in the intention to remain a virgin which in Luke's Gospel underlies her reply to Gabriel. The consecrated virgin is separated from her country and her father's house in a more profound sense than the bride because she leaves not only the particular milieu in which she has lived but even the normal human way of life. This would surely have been the case with Mary because in her time virginity was not yet a customary way of consecration to God. With no precedents to guide and encourage her, she must have been drawn by a divine call and the inspiration of the Holy Spirit.

The initial faith of both Abraham and Mary had to develop through many trials. For Abraham the supreme test came when he was commanded to sacrifice his only son, the child of promise, through whom he was to have a numerous progeny. He could not understand the divine plan behind the cruel order, which seemed to be a negation of the promises so often repeated to him and the destruction of all his hopes. But in complete submission he led his son to the mount of sacrifice; and by this obedience, executed in utter darkness, his faith received its ultimate purification as it gave up the last shred of human support to which it might cling. Abraham was not deprived of his son; but he did have to make a real sacrifice of him in the inner submission to the divine command which called for the son's death.

Mary's faith too was tried by the sacrifice of her Son; and His death actually occurred. She was not asked to accomplish it by her own hand, as Abraham was, but she had to consent to it inwardly by conforming to God's will. Only the purest and firmest faith could survive the death and ignominy of the One Hope of the world and still confidently expect the glorious resurrection. Mary's faith did not need purification, but from this trial it gained, nonetheless, new degrees of intensity and sublimity.

By his faith Abraham became the father of the Jewish people and the father "of many nations" (Gen. 17:6). By her faith Mary became the Second Eve, "the mother of all the living" (Gen. 3:20), the mother of the People of God. It might be argued that Abraham is the father of the Church, since Paul says that "if you are Christ's then you are the offspring of Abraham" (Gal. 3:9). But this fatherhood is metaphorical only whereas Mary's motherhood is really a source of life for her children.

Besides the blessing of a son, Abraham's faith brought him the promise that he would live to an old age and die in peace (Gen. 15:15). Nothing is said to Mary about the end of her life, but in the divine plan that Gabriel announced there was already the intention of bringing her life to a culmination that would surpass Abraham's in glory by as much as her parenthood surpassed his in dignity.

The divine exaltation did not withdraw either Abraham or Mary from the human duty of serving others, as may be noted in one last, dubious parallel between Abraham's going to the rescue of his nephew Lot (Gen. 14) and Mary's going to the aid of her cousin Elizabeth (Luke 1:39).

Mary was not only a direct descendant of Abraham, she was even more akin to him by faith than by her flesh. Though the daughter surpassed the father, she was true to his lineage. Abraham and Mary had analogous roles in the mystery of salvation: he in the beginning, she at its climax. Abraham was a rough type and foreshadowing of the masterpiece which Mary was to be, and what was promised to her was the fulfillment in her of the original promise made to him.

Mary is the Mother of faith because of her belief, which was far greater than that of Abraham, the father of our faith. She is the Mother of our faith, of all the mysteries of revelation to be believed, and she shared in the dispensation of the revealing Word as it unfolded before her for the salvation of the world. In a general audience (May 10, 1967) Pope Paul developed this theme of Mary's faith: "She was assuredly enlightened by a charism of extraordinary faith such as her innocence and her mission were to assure her. The clear knowledge and the prohetic intuition of divine things that flooded her privileged soul were apparent from the gospel. Nevertheless, Our Lady had the faith, which implies not a direct evidence of knowledge, but an acceptance of the truth by reason of the revealing word of God."

The Pope stated that we find confirmation of this primary virtue in Mary in every page where the gospel depicts Mary— what she was, what she said, and what she did. He asked the people to follow her example in this primary virtue—

> We feel ourselves obliged to sit in the school of her example, and find in the attitudes which define the incomparable figure of Mary before the mystery of Christ which is realized in her, the typical patterns for those hearts which wish to be religious, in accordance with the divine plan of our salvation.
>
> These are examples of listening, of exploring, of accepting, of sacrificing; they are furthermore, patterns of meditation, of expectation, and of interrogation, of inner control, of calm and sovereign assurance in judgement and action, and lastly, forms of

fullness in prayer and communion which indeed belong to that unique soul full of grace and enveloped by the Holy Spirit. But they are also examples of faith and therefore close to us, not only to be admired by us, but also to be imitated.

As Mary possessed faith in such a sublime degree, we must ask her for an increase of faith in our own lives—

Let us ask Mary for this supreme gift, that of faith; this gift which today is the more priceless as it is less guarded and valued; this gift which more than any other, gives us the means to liken ourselves to the Virgin in instilling in ourselves that Word of God that became incarnate in her bosom; that gift which from the twilight of this present life is to lead us to the dawn of the eternal day.

While Pope Paul has pointed to Mary as the model of every virtue, she excels in the gift of faith—

O blessed one who believed, who accepted the will of the Omnipotent God. Your soul assented to His proposal and you accepted the reality of Our Lord coming into the world. Your were faithful. This is the never-ending lesson taught us by the Mother of God." [Aug. 15, 1968.]

Such a thought paraphrases the Year of Faith of 1967–68 stressed by Pope Paul and constantly emphasized during his general audiences during the current year. He pleaded for an appreciation of the virtue of faith, for the exercise of it, for its value among Christians today. The model and Mother of our faith is Mary.

Mary's powerful intercession is emphasized strongly in preaching. But other scriptural data which speak of her faith, her perplexity, her inability to grasp the divine plan at the time, and even her apparent rejection by Our Lord are not often spoken of or not as much as they should be. Men cannot imitate the power of her intercession, but they can imitate her faith.

While Mary is the Mother of our faith and led a life of faith, humility, and obedience as the first member of the pilgrim Church, we must not consider her a superhuman being who passed through life untried. She is involved in the history of salvation; she must be. But she is not a being isolated from man. The theology of Mary is a record of personal involvement in the mystery of salvation. As a daughter of Sion, Mary is the person to whom the joy of salvation is made known by the angel. By her consent she is drawn into the plan of salvation in a special, irreplaceable role. Such a role in redemption history is the personal destiny Mary has from God. "She has believed" and is blessed for her faith.

After the occasion at Jerusalem, Jesus "returned with them and came to Nazareth; and He was submissive to them; but His Mother kept all these words in her heart; as for Jesus, He grew in wisdom, in stature, and in grace before God and man" (Luke 2:51-52). This Passover journey marked a turning point in the life and mission of Jesus. The relation of Jesus with the Temple, with the Word of God, and with "His Father's business" is revealed. His messianic mission is awakened, and this is, after the first shock, a new matter for meditation in Mary's heart. The refrain concerning the growth of the Child is repeated: "He grew in stature and wisdom; he grew in the grace of God," and this not only in the mysterious relation with the Father, not only "before God," but also "before men." It seems that with the passing years Christ's wisdom and grace are revealed in a new way to the eyes of those around Him, and particularly of Mary, who little by little sees that the words spoken to her by the Lord at the Annunciation, by Elizabeth at the Visitation, and by Simeon and Anna at the Presentation are coming true; she is indeed the mother of the Son of God.

It is hard to speak and not less hard to think about. The Mother of God was never a theme of the public preaching of the Apostles; while Christ was preached on the housetops, and proclaimed for all to know in an initiatory teaching addressed to the whole world, the mystery of his Mother was revealed only to those who were within the Church . . . . It is not so much an object of faith as a foundation of our hope, a

fruit of faith, ripened in tradition. Let us therefore keep
silence, and let us not try to dogmatize about the supreme
glory of the Mother of God. In the opinion of the Orthodox
theologian V. Lossky such too would be the thought of many
other Orthodox Christians.

To express some of their feeling for Mary, one may cite
this commentary in a recent (1966) liturgical book used by
the Greek Orthodox Church—

> The Virgin Mary, *Theotokos,* did not only serve the Will of God
> in the Incarnation of Jesus Christ, but she was also the eye-
> witness-historian of what took place during the fulfillment of the
> Will of God.
>
> The Eastern Orthodox Church glorifies and magnifies her by
> bestowing on her the highest honor, calling her the *Theotokos,*
> Birth-Giver of God. In the Bible she is mirrored in the *"Magnifi-
> cat"* and in what she kept in her heart; in Icons the Blessed Virgin
> always appears with her Child and never alone; in the hymns of
> the Church her mission is related to her Son's work; in church
> teachings she is described neither as an ordinary woman, even
> after her mission, nor as goddess-like, but as the *Theotokos,* Birth-
> Giver of God, forever. The virgin birth of Jesus Christ, Her Son,
> is a redemptive truth, and her ever-virginity a steadfast belief.
> Her mission was divine; her birth human, being one of her race.
> The Church commemorates her in its hymnology and its prayers.
> It honors her personality and mission in superb prose and poetry,
> officially and otherwise. The Church has recorded her name in its
> redemptive truths and has put it in the Creed.

Typical of the Eastern devotion to Mary is this passage
from the Akathistos hymn. It is used as a kind of litany in
honor of Our Lady by Eastern Christians, Catholic and Orthodox—

> Hail, vessel of the wisdom of God; hail, treasury of
>   His foreknowledge.
> Hail, thou that showest philosphers fools; hail,
>   thou that provest logicians illogical.
> Hail, for the subtle disputants are confounded; hail,
>   for the writers of myths are withered.
> Hail, thou who didst break the webs of the Athenians;
>   hail, thou who didst fill the nets of the fishermen.

Hail, thou who drawest us from the depths of ignorance;
hail, thou who enlightenest many with knowledge.
Hail, raft for those who desire to be saved;
hail, haven for those who swim on the waves of the world.
Hail, thou bride unwedded!

Many Protestant churches observe the feasts of Our Lady, such as those of the Annunciation, the Visitation, her Nativity, and the Assumption. In at least one instance they refer to the "heavenly birthday of Our Lady" for the Feast of the Assumption, or Dormition of Mary. Martin Luther is said to have believed in the Immaculate Conception all his life, though Lutherans today do not subscribe to this belief. The brothers of Taize, who use a liturgy of the Reformed Church, keep only one feast of Our Lady, that of August 15, but they keep it "in memory of" the Virgin Mary. Thus the prayer of the liturgy for August 15 is: "Almighty God, who hast filled with Thy special grace the Blessed Virgin Mary, Mother of Our Lord, sanctify, we beseech Thee, our hearts and our bodies, and grant us like her to live in purity, humility and love, through Jesus Christ, Thy Son, our Lord, who liveth and reigneth with Thee, in the unity of the Holy Spirit, one God world without end. Amen."

The Byzantine liturgy celebrates the Assumption of Mary in this way—

> In thy maternity thou didst retain thy virginity and even though thou hadst ascended to heaven, thou didst not forsake the world: O Mother of God, thou hast passed to life, since thou are the Mother of Life; through thine intercession save our souls from death.
>
> Death and the tomb could not retain the Mother of God, always ready to intercede for us, our unshakable hope and our protection, since she is the Mother of Life, who lifted her up to life, of Christ who dwelt in her ever-virgin womb!
>
> All human generations bless thee, O Mother of God: the laws of nature were overcome in thee, O most pure Virgin, for thy birth-giving was virgin and thy death is a herald of life. O thou didst remain a virgin in thy birth-giving, and who didst remain a life after thy death, O Mother of God, deign to save thine inheritance.

And the Roman liturgy honors Mary in this way on the feast of the Assumption—

> Almighty everlasting God who took up body and soul the immaculate Virgin Mary, Mother of Your Son into heavenly glory, we beseech You that always devoting ourselves to heavenly things, we may be found worthy to share in her glory. Through the same Jesus Christ.

Dr. George Knight writes of Mary as Mother of God in this manner—

> The Virgin Mary is hailed in several branches of the Church as *Theotokos*, the Mother of God. In the light of the above, may we not again conclude that the reality of such a title is to be found rather in her representative capacity as the Church of Israel? It was Israel, we have argued, which was *Theotokos*, and which became the Mother of Christ, though it was sinful, stubborn, backsliding Israel that became such. And surely if we do make the identification we speak of a far greater mystery of love and condescension on the part of the Father than if the term *Theotokos* were to refer only to a single woman who was without sin herself. That is to say, in claiming the title *Theotokos* for the Church we are showing forth a still more holy mystery. It is the mystery that we who by faith are now part of the Body of Christ, and who are joined, through Christ, with Abraham, Isaac and Joseph and Mary that we may share in the mystery of being *Theotokos* ourselves! Thus if we praise Mary as Mother of God, then we are praising ourselves. But if we remember that together with Mary we form the Church of the redeemed, then we can make her son our song, her Magnificat our Magnificat. [*Scottish Theological Quarterly,* Jan., 1966.]

In order that the redemption of mankind be performed as God willed it, by the incarnation of the Word of God ("The Word was made flesh"—John 1:14)—that is, by the birth, life, death, and resurrection upon earth of the Son of God—it was necessary that He should be also truly the Son of man: "God sent His Son, made of a woman" (Gal. 4:4). Jesus Christ is true God and true man: this is the central fact of the Christian faith and was the object of the earliest dogmatic definitions. An essential corollary is the affirmation that the divine and human natures are united in the one Person of Christ, for to deny the unity in the one Person of Christ is to empty His redemptive work of its meaning and value, both divine and human.

This affirmation of the unity of the Person of Christ was the task of the Council of Ephesus in 431, and as we have seen, the affirmation was made in terms of the Blessed Virgin. The first canon of the Council affirms that "the 'Emmanuel' is truly God, and therefore the Holy Virgin is *Theotokos,* for she gave birth according to the flesh to the Word of God made flesh." This proclamation of Mary as Theotokos, "God-bearer," as we now say, "Mother of God," means that Mary is the mother of the one Person, Jesus Christ, who is both true God and true man; consequently she is rightly called the Mother of God.

St. Ignatius of Antioch in the second century, as well as St. Gregory Nazianzen in the fourth and St. Cyril of Alexandria in the fifth, declared that Mary was truly the Mother of God, Theotokos, the expression also appearing later in St. John Cassian, St. Vincent of Lerins, and St. John of Damascus.

The title of Mary as Theotokos was first used among the Greeks at least at the end of the third century (by Alexander of Alexandria, in his epistle to Alexander of Constantinople) and has remained ever since the favorite appellation for her among the Byzantines, both Catholic and Orthodox. Moreover, it places her, as do the gospel and the Creed ("born of the Virgin Mary"), in her proper position in the mystery of the Incarnation and the history of our salvation. That history begins in St. Luke's Gospel with the angel's Ave: "Hail, full of grace, the Lord is with thee . . . the Holy Spirit shall come upon thee . . . and therefore also the Holy which shall be born of thee shall be called the Son of God" (1:28, 35). The conception of Christ in the womb of His mother (commemorated on the Feast of the Annunciation, or "Lady Day," nine months before Christmas) was the work of the Holy Spirit,

God's work initiated for the love of mankind. At the same time the human race was privileged to have a share in it: the angel said, "Behold, thou shalt conceive in your womb and bring forth a son, and thou shalt call his name Jesus" (Luke 1:31).

Mary is the Mother of God. The child she conceived and bore is the Son of God. In His divine nature He existed eternally. But Jesus owed His human nature to Mary as much as any man owes his humanity to his mother. There is nothing that makes my mother mine which is lacking in Mary's relation to Christ as man. As God, He was born of the Father before all ages; as man He was born at a particular moment of time of the Virgin Mary. He was consubstantial with the Father as to His human nature, consubstantial with His Mother in His human nature. It is not sufficient to call her the mother of His human nature, for natures do not have mothers. A mother gives birth to a person. She was the mother of the person born of her. And that Person was God the Son.

A great Greek father, Cyril of Alexandria, protagonist of the Council of Ephesus (431), cited the role of the Mother of God in these terms—

> Hail, Mother of God, venerable treasure of all the world, lamp that is never extinguished, refulgent crown of virginity, indestructible shrine, mother and virgin at once, from you in fact there is born Him of whom the gospel says: "Blessed is he who comes in the name of the Lord."
> This too we should repeat, drawing from our hearts, each by himself and all together the same praise, as a gentle and loving voice for the Blessed Lady that brought to the world the light of salvation. [PG 77:1054.]

St. John of Damascus, who said that the name Theotokos "embraced every mystery of the economy of salvation," writes: "She is all fair and very near to God: for in surpassing the Cherubim and elevated above the Seraphim, she stands close to God," so that "nothing, therefore, in this world can be compared to Mary, Mother of God." The name Mother of God rings a note of faith and hope very frequently in the liturgy, especially that of the Eastern Church. It is sufficient to recall the liturgy of St. John Chrysostom, which was celebrated in St. Peter's while Vatican Council II was in session, in which the term Theotokos occurs frequently. In the rite of preparation before the image of the Virgin, the following troparion is said: "O Mother of God, fountain of mercy, make us worthy of thy compassion; look with kindness upon the sinful people; show, as always, thy power, that we, hoping in thee, may cry unto thee: Hail, as once did Gabriel, the leader of the heavenly hosts."

It is well known that the reformers Luther, Calvin, and Zwingli not only refused to deny the traditional doctrine of the divine maternity of Mary but on several occasions even greatly praised this revealed truth. We may recall the words pronounced by Luther in 1521, in his explanation of the Magnificat—

> In this dispensation in which she has become the Mother of God, so many and such great gifts have been granted her that they surpass all understanding. And this is why all honor and blessedness follow her and why in all humankind there is but one person above all the rest, in comparison to whom there is no other, since with the Heavenly Father she has one Son—and so great a Son. Thus, when one says "Mother of God," with this one title all her glory is expressed, nor can anyone predicate more of her, even if he were to have as many tongues as the leaves of the trees, and the blades of grass, the stars of the firmament, and the grains of sand on the seashore. And in our hearts we must ponder just what this means: to be the Mother of God.

According to Catholic teaching, Mary was a virgin before, during, and after the birth of Christ. She conceived by the Holy Spirit without the cooperation of man and bore her Son without threat to her virginity in any way. Remaining a virgin her entire life, she was finally assumed body and soul into heaven.

Aristides very clearly refers to the virgin birth, and both St. Irenaeus and Tertullian dwell upon it at considerable length. It occurs in St. Hippolytus and Lactantius, and in the fourth century in St. Gregory Nazianzen and in St. Jerome's *The Perpetual Virginity of Blessed Mary.* In the post-Nicene period the principal witnesses are St. Augustine, St. Peter Chrysologus, St. Leo the Great, and finally St. John of Damascus.

Tertullian is the first to emphasize that Mary was a virgin during Christ's birth, and the assertion is repeated later in the usual writers—St. Gregory Nazianzen, St. Augustine, St. Peter Chrysologus, St. Leo the Great, and St. John of Damascus. The same writers, along with St. Jerome, attest Mary's perpetual virginity.

In St. Cyril of Alexandria we find—

Christ, as I have said, was also God in his humanity, permitting human nature to use its laws while nonetheless conserving also the purity of divinity. For in this way and in no other is God to be understood both what was born of nature, and those things which the Virgin Mother produced not only of flesh and blood in the same way that other mothers do, but [the flesh and blood] of the Lord and of God imbued with our likeness. [*Paschal Homilies,* No. 17:2 *MG* 77, 776.]

For [Paul], writing to the Galatians, says: "God sent His own Son made of a woman" [Gal. 4:4], who of course is admitted to have been a virgin, although Hebion resists [this doctrine]. I recognize, too, the Angel Gabriel as having been sent to a "virgin." But when he is blessing her, it is "among women," not among virgins, that he ranks her: "Blessed art thou among women" [Luke 1:28]. For the angel knew that even a virgin is called a woman. Here, at all events, there can be no semblance of speaking prophetically as if the apostle should have named a future woman, that is, bride, in saying "made of a woman." For he could not be naming a posterior woman, from whom Christ had not to be born that is, one who had known a man; but she who was then present, who was a virgin, in accordance with the primordial norm, [as belonging] to a virgin, and thus to the universal class of women." [*On the Veiling of Virgins,* ch. 6, *ML* 2, 897.]

God recovered his own image and likeness, of which he had been robbed by the devil. For it was while Eve was yet a virgin, that the ensnaring word had crept into her ear which was to build the edifice of death. Into a virgin's soul, in like manner, must be introduced that Word of God which was to raise the fabric of life; so that what had been reduced to ruin by this sex might, by the selfsame sex be recovered to salvation. As Eve had believed the serpent, so Mary believed the angel. The delinquency which the one occasioned by believing, the other by believing effaced. [*On the Flesh of Christ,* ch. 17, *ML* 2, 782.]

For who was more worthily to perform the initiatory rite on the body of the Lord, than flesh similar in kind to that which conceived and gave birth to that [body]? And indeed it was a virgin, about to marry once for all after her delivery, who gave birth to Christ, in order that each title of sanctity might be fulfilled in Christ's parentage, by means of a mother who was both virgin, and wife of one husband. [*On Monogamy,* ch 8, *ML* 2, 939.]

St. Ephraim of Syria: "Truly you, Lord, and your mother are the only ones who are beautiful, completely so in every respect; for, Lord, there is no spot in you, not any soot at all in your mother." (*Nisibene Hymns,* 27 *BK* 122).

In general this chapter section does not manifest any new Marian concept or development over the past generation or so. Much attention has been given to Mary's role in salvation and to her spiritual motherhood of the redeemed, especially from papal statements going back to Pope Pius X. At present there seems to be a more critical evaluation of papal teaching. They are surely authoritative statements but are not necessarily to be given the strength of the magisterium previously accorded.

I do not wish to give the impression of playing down the special character of papal teaching, but at the same time I wish to say that the words of a pope in a letter or in an allocution are not intended to finalize a position of theology so that no further discussion is possible. Then, too, the popes have at times written and spoken in a way that is poetical rather than rigorously theological.

St. Gregory Nazienzen (329–389), one of the greatest of the Greek fathers, writes in terms of the Lord's Ascension—

It is the risen Christ who sets us free from our sins, Christ, ascending to heaven to assure for everyone of us a throne of glory there. And we have holy Church, our Mother on this earth, inspired by the Spirit of Jesus and by the undying flame of the apostolate of

her children, called to spiritual conquests in this world. Finally we
have Mother, taken body and soul into heaven where she has become the loving object of our aspirations, our devotion, and filial
affection, Mary who invites us to imitate her virtues and those of
the saints in heaven.

The importance of the Assumption of Mary for Protestants
has been noted by Dr. George Knight—

What, finally, are Protestants to say about the doctrine of the
Assumption? I believe we can say something that is really positive,
for we can do so on the basis of the biblical realism about the
Incarnation. The New Testament's insistence that the word did
not just "clothe itself" in flesh, but actually became flesh, egeneto,
is a truth that demands our taking the word "flesh" seriously. Since
the birth of Jesus was of the Holy Spirit and of the flesh of Mary,
then Jesus received his body from Mary. We recall that the Old
Testament knows no separation between what we sometimes call
"matter" and what we call "spirit." This means that the human
nephesh, as the Old Testament understands, is to be regarded as
one entity. A man is, in fact, his body.

We recall John Calvin's succinct word: "There is a man in
heaven." That man is the body that walked the roads of Galilee.
After the Resurrection He still remained that body. "See my hands
and my feet," he declared to Thomas. Then came the Ascension.

Though many of us employ demythologising language when we
speak of the Ascension, we dare not by-pass the reality behind the
myth. The reality is, then, quite simply "There is a man in heaven."
And that man is the body He received from His Mother. And His
Mother is Israel.

The doctrine of the Assumption can mean for both Roman
Catholic and Protestant the unspeakable mystery, that, though God
does not change and is the same yesterday, today and forever, yet
He assumed unto Himself, in Christ, the flesh which He Himself
created and called to serve and praise Him in the form of the
Covenant People. This mystery in itself is sufficient to hold us together in thoughtful dialogue with our Roman Catholic brethren
as far into the future as we can see. [*Scottish Theological Quarterly.*]

Pope John XXIII expressed his thoughts on Mary's assumption into heavenly glory—

The greatest mission which began with the angel's announcement to Mary has passed like a stream of fire and light through all the Mysteries in turn: God's eternal plan for our salvation has been presented to us in one scene after another, accompanying us along our way and now it brings us back to God in the spendour of heaven.

He said that the triumph of Mary is the triumph of Jesus, and he explained—

Jesus is the real conqueror. The queenly figure of Mary is illuminated and glorified in the highest dignity which a creature may attain. What grace and solemnity in the scene of Mary's falling asleep as the Christians of the East imagine it. She is lying in the supreme sleep of death; Jesus stands beside her and clasps her soul, as it were a tiny child, to His heart, to indicate the miracle of her immediate resurrection and glorification.

The same Pope made the Assumption of Mary the type of the resurrection of each member of Christ—

The mystery of the Assumption brings home to us the thought of death, of our death, and gives us a sense of serene confidence; it makes us understand and welcome the thought that the Lord will be, as we wish Him to be, near us in our last agony, together into His own hands our immortal soul. "May your grace be always with us, Immaculate Virgin."

Next to Christ, Mary recapitulates in herself all the values of history from the time of Adam, all that in the vision of God was meaningful in the history of nations, in Abraham, in Israel, and in Sion.

In Mary, taken up to heavenly glory both in body and in soul, the Church sees its own consummation. In her, the queen of the universe, there shines forth all that likeness to Christ which grace gives to men. For grace makes man like Christ, conformable to His image (Rom. 8:29), and it makes him sit with Christ on a royal throne (Apoc. 3:21). Mary shows forth in a unique way the effect of the Redemption.

In this final paragraph about the Assumption there is an allusion to the Immaculate Conception. Neither doctrine is strictly biblical; they are not stressed in this section, nor are they left unmentioned. The document uses the words of Pope Pius XII in the definition of 1950: "Finally preserved free from all guilt of original sin, the immaculate Virgin was taken up body and soul into heaven glory and upon the completion of her earthly sojourn." It also refers to the same Pope about the queenship of Mary, who partakes of the glory of heaven with her Son: "She was exalted by the Lord as Queen of all, in order that she might be the more thoroughly conformed to her Son, the Lord of lords [cf. Apoc. 19:16] and the conqueror of sin and death."

A century ago the Church made the Marian doctrine of the Immaculate Conception the subject of an infallible definition. For century upon century before that, Catholics had held it for certain truth, for once the Church had formulated with all possible clearness the doctrines of the Trinity and the Incarnation, so that Catholics could live day in and day out in full awareness of who and what Christ is, they began to see it as unthinkable that He should have allowed His mother to exist for any time at all without sanctifying grace. Yet for many devoted lovers of the Blessed Virgin a disturbing question remained. Our Lady had said in the Magnificat, "My spirit rejoices in God my Saviour." How could God be her Saviour, what was there to save her from, if she had had grace always?

But there is one special element in Christ's power to give that we might easily overlook. Because He was God, He could give His mother gifts, not only before He was born of her but before she was born herself. This is the meaning of the doctrine of the Immaculate Conception.

It is surprising how this phrase has caught the non-Catholic imagination, but more surprising how, for the non-Catholic who uses it, it has little trace of its true meaning. Ninety-nine times out of a hundred it is used to mean the virgin birth of Christ. It does not, however, refer to Christ's conception in

Mary's womb; it refers to Mary's conception in the womb of her own mother. Nor does it mean that she was virginally conceived: she had a father and a mother. It means that her Son's care for her and His gifts to her began from the first moment of her existence.

For all of us, conception comes when God creates a soul and unites it with the bodily element formed in the mother's womb. But from the very first moment of its creation, Mary's soul had, by God's gift, not natural life only but also supernatural life. What this means quite simply is that she whom God chose to be His mother never existed for an instant without sanctifying grace in her soul.

In other words, does the Orthodox Church agree with the Roman Catholic doctrine of the Immaculate Conception, proclaimed as a dogma by Pope Pius IX in 1854, according to which Mary, from the moment she was conceived by her mother St. Anne, was by God's special decree delivered from "all stain of original sin"? The Orthodox Church has never in fact made any formal and definitive pronouncement on the matter. In the past, individual Orthodox have surely believed in the Immaculate Conception, and they can quote in their support texts from the Greek Fathers and the liturgical books; but since 1854 the great majority of Orthodox have rejected the doctrine as defined because they feel the definition unnecessary. They feel that this doctrine, at any rate as defined by the Roman Catholic Church, implies a false understanding of original sin; they suspect the doctrine because it seems to separate Mary from the rest of the descendants of Adam, putting her in a completely different class from all the other righteous men and women of the Old Testament. From the Orthodox point of view, however, the whole question belongs to the realm of theological opinion; and if an individual Orthodox today felt impelled to believe in the Immaculate Conception, he could not be called a heretic for so doing.

In the final article (59) we have the nexus of the mystery of Christ and the mystery of the Church. Mary figured in the preparations for Pentecost—the solemn manifestation of "the

mystery of salvation of the human race," when the Holy Spirit,
who made the Word incarnate in Mary, filled the Church with
the life of Christ. The mystery of salvation means not merely
the mysterious character of Redemption but also the concrete
form that it takes in the visible Church. In three instances
before (arts. 1, 9, 38) the Constitution called the Church the
sacrament of salvation. Mary is included in the solemn proclamation of this sacrament.

It joins the mysteries of the Annunciation and of Pentecost. In both the Holy Spirit has a special role: ". . . we see
the apostles before the day of Pentecost 'continuing with one
mind in prayer with the women and Mary, the Mother of Jesus,
and with His brethren' [Acts 1:14]. We see Mary prayerfully
imploring the gift of the Spirit who had already overshadowed
her in the Annunciation." The Holy Spirit came upon Mary
when she consented to the incarnation of the Word; the Holy
Spirit came upon Mary in a special way when the Church
was to be proclaimed to the world, when the mission and
message of Christ were to be preached to all men. Thus Mary
bears a special relation to the Church of Jesus, even as she
had a unique relation with Him and was bound by an inseparable bond to Him and to His work of salvation.

As a concluding thought and in summary I should like to
refer to these words of praise in honor of our Lady from the
heart of St. John Chrysostom (347–407), famous preacher
and heroic archbishop of Constantinople—

The Son of God did not choose for His Mother a rich or wealthy
woman, but that blessed Virgin whose soul was adorned with
virtues. For it was because the blessed Mary had observed chastity
in a way that was above all human nature that she conceived
Christ the Lord in her womb. Let us then fly to this most Holy Virgin
and Mother of God and avail ourselves of her patronage. Therefore, let all of you who are virgins flee to the Mother of the Lord;
for she, by her patronage, will guard in you that beautiful, precious and incorruptible possession.

The Blessed Mary, ever a virgin, was in truth a great wonder.
For what greater or more wonderful one has ever at any time been
discovered? She alone is greater far than heaven and earth. What is

holier than she? Not the prophets, or apostles, or martyrs, or patriarchs, not the angels, or the thrones of the denominations or the seraphim or the cherubim; in truth no creature whatever, whether visible or invisible, is to be found greater or more excellent than she. She is at once the handmaid of God, and His Mother, at once a Virgin and a parent.

She is the Mother of Him who was begotten of the Father before the beginning of all things; whom angels and men acknowledge to be the Lord of all things. Would you know how much greater is this virgin than any of the heavenly powers? They stand in His presence with fear and trembling and veiled faces; she offers human nature to Him whom she brought forth. Through her we obtain the forgiveness of our sins.

Hail then, O Mother, heaven, maiden, virgin, throne, ornament, glory and foundation of our Church, pray without ceasing for us to Jesus, your Son and our Lord that through you we many find mercy in the day of judgment and may be able to obtain those things which are prepared for those who love God, through the grace and loving-kindness of Jesus Christ our Lord: to whom with the first of those events which were to be the greatest of all time.

The life of Mary must be seen in the context of the life and mission of Jesus, her Son, not apart from Him and surely never in conflict with Him. Mary derives her holiness from Him. She must be seen and interpreted only in relation to Him. She has been given grace and glory because of Him. She is the mother of such a Son, incarnate through her, but chosen by Him for the holy purpose of the world's redemption and His manifestation to all men.

The Marian chapter now turns to a correlative of this role of Jesus and Mary in history: the role of Mary in the Church.

3

THE BLESSED VIRGIN
AND THE CHURCH
(60-65)

60. We have but one Mediator, as we know from the words of the Apostle: "For there is one God, and one Mediator between God and men, himself man, Christ Jesus, who gave himself as ransom for all . . ." [I Tim. 2:5-6]. The maternal duty of Mary toward men in no way obscures or diminishes this unique mediation of Christ, but rather shows its power. For all the saving influences of the Blessed Virgin on men originate, not from some inner necessity, but from the divine pleasure. They flow forth from the superabundance of the merits of Christ, rest on His mediation, depend entirely on it, and draw all their power from it. In no way do they impede the immediate union of the faithful with Christ. Rather, they foster this union.

61. The Blessed Virgin was eternally predestined, in conjunction with the incarnation of the divine Word, to be the Mother of God. By decree of the divine Providence, she served on earth as the loving Mother of the divine Redeemer, an associate of unique nobility, and the Lord's humble handmaid. She presented Him to the Father in the temple, and was united with Him in suffering as He died on the cross. In an utterly singular way she cooperated by her obedience, faith, and hope and burning charity in the Saviour's work of restoring supernatural life to souls. For this reason she is a mother to us in the order of grace.

62. This maternity of Mary in the order of grace began with the consent which she gave in faith at the Annunciation and which she sustained without wavering beneath the cross. This maternity will last without interruption until the eternal fulfillment of all the select. For, taken up to heaven, she did not lay aside this saving

role, but by her manifold acts of intercession continues to win for us gifts of eternal salvation.[1]

By her maternal charity, Mary cares for the brethren of her Son who still journey on earth surrounded by dangers and difficulties, until they are led to their happier fatherland. Therefore the Blessed Virgin is invoked by the Church under the titles of Advocate, Auxiliatrix, Adjutrix, and Mediatrix.[2]

These, however, are to be so understood[3] that they neither take away from nor add anything to the dignity and efficacy of Christ the one Mediator.[4]

For no creature could ever be classed with the Incarnate Word and Redeemer. But, just as the priesthood of Christ is shared in various ways both by sacred ministers and by the faithful, and as the one goodness of God is in reality communicated diversely to His creatures, as also the unique mediation of the Redeemer does not exclude but rather gives rise among creatures to a manifold cooperation which is but a sharing in this unique source.

The Church does not hesitate to profess this subordinate role of Mary. She experiences it continuously and commends it to the hearts of the faithful, so that encouraged by this material help they may more closely adhere to the Mediator and Redeemer.

63. Through the gift and role of divine maternity, Mary is united with her Son, the Redeemer, and with His singular graces and offices.

By these the Blessed Virgin is also intimately united with the Church. As St. Ambrose taught, the Mother of God is a model of the Church[5] in the matter of faith, charity, and perfect union

---

[1] Cf. Kleutgen, the revised text of *De mysterio Verbi incarnati*, c. IV: *Mansi*, 53, 290. Cf. St. Andrew of Crete, *In nat. Mariae, Sermo 4*: PG 97, 865A; St. Germanus of Constantinople, *In Annunt. Deiparae*: PG 98, 321 BC, and his *In dorm. B.V. Mariae*, Hom. 1, 8: PG 96, 712BC-712A, and *In Dorm. Deiparae*, III, PG 98, 361D.

[2] Cf. Leo XIII, encyclical *Adiutricem populi*, Sept. 5, 1895: *Acta Sanctae Sedis 15* (1895-96), p. 303: St. Pius X, encyclical *Ad diem illum*, Feb. 2, 1904: *Pii X Pontificis Maximi Acta*, I, p. 154 (*Denz.* 1978 a/3370/). Pius XII, radio message, May 13, 1946: *AAS*, 38 (1946), p. 178; Pius XI, encyclical, Miserentissimus, May 8, 1928: *AAS*, 20 (1928), 178.

[3] The Council applies to the Blessed Virgin the title of mediatrix, but carefully explains this so as to remove any impression that it could detract from the uniqueness and sufficiency of Christ's position as Mediator (cf. I Tim. 2:5), already referred to in chap. 1 (art. 8).

[4] St. Ambrose *Epist.*, 63: PL 16, 1218.

[5] The theme of Mary as type of the Church, developed in this and the following two articles, in central to the chapter and partly accounts for the decision of the Council to treat Mariology in the Constitution on the Church.

with Christ[6] For in the mystery of the Church, herself rightly called mother and virgin, the Blessed Virgin stands out in eminent and singular fashion as exemplar of both virginity and motherhood.[7]

For, believing and obeying, Mary brought forth on earth the Father's Son. This she did, knowing not man but overshadowed by the Holy Spirit. She was the new Eve, who put her absolute trust not in the ancient serpent but in God's messenger. The Son whom she brought forth is He whom God placed as the first-born among many brethren [cf. Rom. 8:29], namely the faithful. In their birth and development she cooperates with a maternal love.

64. The Church, moreover, contemplating Mary's mysterious sanctity, imitating her charity, and faithfully fulfilling the Father's will, becomes herself a mother by accepting God's word in faith. For by her preaching and by baptism she brings forth a new and immortal life children who are conceived of the Holy Spirit and born of God. The Church herself is a virgin, who keeps whole and pure the fidelity she has pledged to her Spouse. Imitating the Mother of her Lord, and by the power of the Holy Spirit, she preserves with virginal purity and integral faith, a firm hope, and a sincere charity.[8]

65. In the most holy Virgin the Church has already reached that perfection whereby she exists without spot or wrinkle [cf. Eph. 5:27]. Yet the followers of Christ still strive to increase in holiness by conquering sin. And so they raise their eyes to Mary who shines forth to the whole community of the elect as a model of the virtues. Devotedly meditating on her and contemplating her in the light of the Word made man, the Church with reverence enters more intimately into the supreme mystery of the Incarnation and becomes ever increasingly like her Spouse.

For Mary figured profoundly in the history of salvation and in a certain way unites and mirrors within herself the central truths of the faith. Hence when she is being preached and venerated, she summons the faithful to her Son and His sacrifices, and to love for the Father. Seeking after the glory of Christ, the Church becomes more like her exalted model and continually progresses in

---

6 St. Ambrose, *Expos. Lc.*, II, 7: PL 15, 1555.

7 Cf. pseudo-Peter Damian, *Serm.*, 63: PL 144, 861As; Godfrey of St. Victor, *In nat. B.M.* Ms. Paris, Mazarine, 1002, fol. 109r; Gerhoh of Reichersberg, *De gloria et honore filii hominis*, 10: PL 194, 1105AB.

8 St. Ambrose as cited in footnote 6, as well as his *Expos. Lc.*, X, 24-25: PL 15, 1810; St. Augustine, *In Io.*, tr. 13, 12: PL 35, 1499, and see also his *Serm.*, 191, 2,3,: PL 38, 1010, as well as other of his texts. Cf. Venerable Bede, *In Lc. Expos.*, I, c. 2: PL 92, 330; *Isaac of Stella, Ser.*, 51: PL 194, 1863A.

faith, hope, and charity, searching out and doing the Will of God in all things. Hence the Church in her apostolic work also rightly looks to her who brought forth Christ, conceived by the Holy Spirit and born of the Virgin, so that through the Church Christ may be born and grow in the hearts of the faithful also. The Virgin Mary in her own life lived an example of that maternal love by which all should be fittingly animated who cooperated in the apostolic mission of the Church on behalf of the rebirth of men.

In the original draft the key thought of this section was "mediatrix." The meaning of that term brought forth spirited clashes in the Council, and though the concept is developed, for example in accord with Mary's mediation, the term itself is not used, except in an offhand way. For some this term is as objectionable as "co-redemptrix." Others felt that its use would cause difficulties in regard to ecumenism. So there was the compromise: to develop clearly the notion of Marian mediation without using the term mediatrix.

At the very outset the truth quoted from St. Paul that there is only one mediator between God and men should help to preclude the mistaken idea that Catholic belief somehow sets up a separate and efficacious mediator together with Christ, or in place of Him. This Pauline text had occurred later on in the previous version of the schema was but moved forward to set the tone of all that follows. Catholic belief does not consider this text a thorny one to be explained away; indeed, it bases Mary's whole position squarely on the unique mediation of Christ. It is the function of grace to raise men to share in the Saviour's theandric being and redemptive activity. The grace that a person receives in himself becomes a source of or aid to salvation for his brethren. This is especially and uniquely so in the case of Mary. She originally received into herself the source of all life and is thereby the spiritual mother of all the other members of the Church.

Mary's spiritual motherhood or mediation consists of two elements: her association with the historical Christ; and the continuance at the present time and until the end of the world of her spiritual motherly care of all the members of Christ.

In this matter two dogmatic extremes are to be avoided:

(1) the belief that she simply consented to the Incarnation and continued her life of faith and love until His death; and (2) the belief that she continues her mediation in heaven in exactly the same way as she did on earth—in a kind of historical activity on a higher plane.

Though I mentioned Mary's mediation somewhat in the last section, I should refer to it again because of the specific mention of the title mediatrix, together with advocate, auxiliatrix, and adjutrix (art. 62). "These, however, are to be so understood that they neither take away from nor add anything to the dignity and efficacy of Christ the one Mediator." The term mediatrix can be accurately interpreted, but it can also be misunderstood, and it would seem that though mention is made of it, there is no detailed exposition of it. Both Pius XII and John XXIII had been cautious in using the title; but to ignore it altogether might be taken as diminishing Mary's honor and a refusal to express what was implicitly in the Constitution. Advocate was used by St. Irenaeus; the next two titles, auxiliatrix and adjutrix, are used by the Eastern churches, while mediatrix as a special title is relatively new in the Church. It was promoted by Cardinal Mercier of Belgium (d. 1928) and taken up with fervor by various Marian congresses and societies in modern times.

The subordinate mediation of Mary, which, as the document has it, the Church constantly experiences, freely acknowledges and commends to the faithful that they may use her motherly aid to adhere intimately to their one Mediator and Saviour. Mary is the partner and associate of her Son in the work of salvation. She did not add to His sacrifice of love, since she did not in any possible way redeem the Word, but rather united her suffering and sorrow with His, in perfect faith and love. Then, to help those Christians who find real difficulty in acknowledging that a human being can have any share in carrying out God's plan of salvation (two parallel cases are adduced): the one priesthood of Christ shared both by ministers and the people of God, and the unique goodness of God spread abroad in various ways among creatures.

When a man dies, his history with all that it meant for himself and for others passes into eternity in the presence of God, showing itself as an intercessory power as it shares in the redemptive work of Christ with which his life was connected. Just as Christ the eternal priest stands before God with His work of salvation, pleading His sacrifice in man's behalf (Heb. 8-10) as our constant intercessor (Heb. 7:25) and advocate (John 2:1), so Mary's share in the redemptive work of Christ—and that of the other saints in their own way—continues intercessory existence before God.

Mary acts as intercessor for men in heaven because she was associated with Christ and His work; what she did on earth with Christ and His work is presented to the Father as a mother's concern for the brethren of her son who are still on pilgrimage to their fatherland. It is under this intercessory presence in heaven that the Church invokes her under the titles of advocate, auxiliatrix, adjutrix, and mediatrix.

Mary is not placed on the same level with Christ. Instead, for the sake of men and for her own salvation she is raised to share in the redemptive work of Christ as saints and all men are raised up because of God's pardon and redemption to share in the life and in the mission of the Church. We may also say that the difference between Christ and Mary is illustrated by the difference between the ordained priest, Christ's official representative, and those possessed of the general priesthood in the Church: Mary's mediation belongs on the level of that spiritual solidarity of all the redeemed but not on the level of the Lord's mediation.

Mary was associated with her Son on earth, cooperating with Him "by her obedience, faith and hope and burning charity in the Saviour's work of restoring supernatural life to souls." The grace of Christ the Head of the Mystical Body is poured out upon her in a special way: "For this reason she is a mother to us in the order of grace."

An ancient tradition, first expressed by St. Ambrose, holds that Mary is the archetype of the Church. It would seem that even the woman of the Apocalypse, chapter 12, is meant to represent the Church. Some would say that the figure represents the Church of the Old Testament, now perfected in the New under the figure of Mary. However, Mary and the Church are typically associated together from early times because both are typically associated with the First Eve.

The idea conveyed in John 19:34 that the Church, based above all on the sacraments of Baptism and the Eucharist, proceeds like a new Eve from the side of the Second Adam is supplemented as early as the second century by the idea that Mary is also an antitype of the First Eve. This connection of the Church and Mary with Eve can be interpreted to mean that Mary and the Church are also connected with each other as type and antitype. Indeed, the Church does not have Mary as a mere image that she resembles: she is the very embodiment of herself. In the consent of Mary to conceive the Word in her body and in her heart, she is the realization and the type of the community who hear and obey the Word of God.

The last three articles of this section (63–5) discuss Mary as the type of the Church without using the term. The first considers her as the archetype, the model of faith and love and perfect union with Christ. The second shows the Church as the antitype of Mary, virgin and mother, imitating the mother of the Lord. The third considers men as the embodiment of this antitype as they are gathered together in the Church.

Mary is the archetype of the Church, so that every grace with which the Church is endowed is found in her. Mary is a mother, and the Church is a mother. Mary is a virgin, as is the Church. The virginal conception and birth continue in her perpetual virginity, in faith and obedience to Jesus and His mission. The interest and concern of Mary for His work make her the spiritual mother of the men He has redeemed; He is the first-born of many brethren. She is the mother of the "whole Christ" head and members, while she herself is a member of Christ.

Mary shows what the Church is by her motherly character. The fruitfulness of Mary is mirrored in the Church, which gives birth by grace to new members of Christ and by its

preaching and the sacraments enables its children to share in
the life of Christ. The assent of faith is not just an intellectual
response to a set of propositions but a surrender of the entire
person to revealed truth, mind and heart and will, for the love
of God. Faith means acceptance of the communication of
God in Christ. Holding to the faith means a personal surrender
to what the Lord has said, to the God who has said it and who
communicates Himself by virtue of His revelation. As Mary
lived by faith, so does the Church; as Mary manifests Christ
to the world, so does the Church. As Mary was the chosen
instrument of salvation, inseparably united to Christ, so also
is the Church.

Mary is the image of the Church by her faithfulness to
grace. In Mary is the perfect realization of what the Church
seeks to become, the ideal to be achieved. This does not mean
that Mary takes the place of Christ as the model of the Christian life, any more than Paul does when he asks the churches
to imitate his example (I Cor. 4:16, 11:1; Phil. 3:17). By
leading a life in imitation of Mary, the Church becomes more
like Christ.

The apostolic mission of the Church is reflected in Mary's
life and character. It is the mission of the Church to bring
Christ to men, even as Mary bore Him for the world. By
apostolic work I mean all the activity by which the Church is
fruitful for men. When the Church communicates supernatural
life, it is an antitype of Mary. By apostolic work I mean not
an office but a function, a duty of each one of the faithful,
and so the Church may look to Mary as archetype in this
motherly fecundity.

I should like to stress Mary's relation to the Church, a
topic for which the Church fathers had a special fondness.
Then I wish to develop thought on the title and concept of
Mary as Mother of the Church.

Mary's life is in itself a résumé of salvation history from
its beginning to its fulfillment. She is immaculate in order to
be the perfect, the most excellent, mother of the Redeemer.
She receives Him in faith, through the overshadowing of the

Holy Spirit; she manifests the Incarnate Word to the world; she lives by obedience, faith, and humility and achieves her destiny of the elect of God. She is the Church in its perfection. Her life on earth was as the Church in history, on its way of pilgrimage. She is the example and exemplar of the people of God, sustaining and encouraging them in their journey to the Father. Mary is the icon of the Church.

Mathias Scheeben, German theologian of the last century, saw the relation of Mary and the Church in this light—

> In general there exists between Mary's motherhood and that of the Church so close, complete and mutual a relation, rather so intrinsic a connection that one can be known only in and with each other. The two are connected and resemble each other by the very fact that they depend upon the Holy Spirit for their fecundity and life, and are therby intended to communicate a holy and spiritual life. In both cases, moreover, the spirtual motherhood over the redeemed includes a motherhood over Christ Himself and indeed owes its perfection to this factor. For, all other maternal functions of the Church center round that by which she brings forth in her womb the Eucharistic Christ as Head, the sacrifice, and the food of the members of His Mystical Body. But the very fact reveals very specially the more sublime and fundamental character of Mary's motherhood in comparison with that of the Church and at the same time the morganic connection between the two, as a result of which the Church's maternal activity is exerted because of and by virtue of Mary's motherhood while Mary carries on her maternal work in and through the Church. [*Mariology*, II, 251.]

The mystery of Mary can help us to understand the mystery of the Church. Or as Father Joseph Ratizinger of Tübingen, Germany, has written—

> It seems to me that the inclusion of the figure of the Mother of God can also shed some light on the mystery of the Church. She exemplifies the paradox of grace that touches those who cannot accomplish anything by themselves. She personifies the Church of the poor, the Church that moves through history as a humble servant, and by that very fact is in a position to express the mystery of God's promise and proximity. Mary also embodies the Church that sprang from the foot of Israel and that carries the hope of

the world that secretly lives beneath its heart through the strenuous journey through history. Thus the decision in the matter of Mariology did open the way to something positive. It may have brought us nearer the time when it will again be conceivable that Christians of different denominations will understand one another on this particularly divisive issue. [*Theological Highlights of Vatican II*, p. 60.]

It is indeed one of the principal differences between Catholicism and the Lutheran and Calvinist forms of Protestantism that these confessions exclude the cooperation of creatures, be they saints in heaven or Christians still living on earth, from the work of salvation; hence their objection to the intercession of the saints in general and the mediation of the Blessed Virgin in particular. True, this mediation has at times been exaggerated by certain Catholics who asserted that it could be exercised even in opposition to the will of her Son, who was bound to "obey" His mother. But such an interpretation is absolutely excluded by the unequivocal terms of the Constitution, which calls Mary's position in this respect "subordinate" and emphasizes the uniqueness of the mediation of Christ, which is the root and source of Mary's own intercessory powers. But within these limits Mary too exercises her mediating activity, of which the Church has experience and which it commends to the faithful so that, as the Constitution is careful to point out, "they may cling the more closely to the mediator and saviour."

After briefly referring to the patristic teaching on Mary as the type of the Church, the Constitution emphasizes that "in the most holy Virgin the Church has already reached that perfection by which she exists without spot or wrinkle." The Christians here on earth still have to battle with sin, and in this battle Mary will be for them the pattern of virtue which they will strive to imitate. Nevertheless, even here Mary is not the final goal of the Church's meditation; but through her Christians will be introduced ever more deeply to the mystery of the Incarnation and thus be more likened to Christ her spouse.

St. Bede writes: "Philip of Harveng never tires of extolling the maternal activity of Mary in the first ages of the Church, bringing forth the apostles, as if bearing them, out of the darkness of ignorance, bringing them up and forming them, and, as the mother of all presiding over them, and through her constancy in faith, calling the vacillating disciples to order."

Mary is the Mother of God. She is the Mother of the Church and the pre-eminent member of the Mystical Body of her Son. It is through her that God planned and effected His renewal of the entire earth and all mankind. She was involved in God's plan of salvation; she was committed as no other creature in all history to the salvific plan of her incarnate Son and the world's Redeemer.

"The glories of Mary are for the sake of her Son." So wrote Cardinal Newman. His words sum up the Church's understanding of the role of Mary in salvation. They explain too the devotion to her that has marked Christian life from the very beginning.

To speak of Mary is to speak of the truth of the Incarnation, not simply as an event in time, long ago, but continued and mediated to men through the Church. Mary is the woman of our race who gave her willing affirmation to God the expression of her all-out love. She is the type and image of the Church, which continues to make Christ present and real to the world and in the world.

"Do whatever he tells you," she said to the servants at Cana. She speaks to us still, she leads our response to God, for no one was closer to God than she.

Dr. Arthur Piepkorn of Concordia Lutheran Seminary, St. Louis, rightly affirms that in our discussion on Mary we must consider the opinions and judgments only of those who affirm the divinity of Christ. If Jesus is not the Son of God, then there is little point, it seems, in discussing Our Lady as His mother.

The distinguished Heidelberg church historian Baron Hans Varon von Compenshausen argues that the primitive Church never knew a Mariology in the strict sense. I quite agree. The formulation of other teachings on the Trinity, the Incarnation the Redemption, were surely not formulated in the early Church in the same way as in later centuries or as they are today. But this fact does not lessen Mary's role in the incarnate life of Christ and in the development of the pristine Church.

The attitude of the Church toward Mary, that attitude of reverent study and imitation, is the most striking indication of the unique place which Mary holds. In Mary the Church sees the perfection "without spot or wrinkle" (Eph. 5:27) which the Church itself strives to reach and teach others. To Mary the Church will always direct the eyes of the faithful; in her it will always point to the achieved model of all vocations to holiness. In its study of the mysteries of the Incarnation and the Redemption, which it is its mission to proclaim to every generation, it will see them revealed in Mary. "For Mary," says the Constitution, "figured profoundly in the history of salvation." Even in its apostolic outlook the Church "rightly looks to her who brought forth Christ, conceived by the Holy Spirit and born of the Virgin so that through the Church Christ might be born and grow in the heart of the faithful also."

Many figures of speech are applied both to Mary and to the Church—Ark of the Covenant, Gate of Heaven, Refuge of Sinners, and the like. Both are mothers who bring forth Christ. In the baptistery of the church of St. John Lateran in Rome an inscription reads: ". . . at this spring the Church our mother bears in her virginal womb the sons whom she has conceived under the breath of God." The same may be said of Mary.

In his commentary on Luke (2:5), St. Ambrose explained: "Rightly is she betrothed, yet a virgin, because she is the type of the Church, which is immaculate [i.e., virginal], yet married. The virgin Church was conceived us by the Spirit, the virgin brings us forth without pain. And therefore perhaps is the holy Mary married to one [Joseph], but filled with another [the Holy Spirit], because the individual Churches, too, are filled by the Spirit and his grace, but are externally joined to a mortal priest [i.e., their bishop]." Thus Mary and the Church are almost interchangeable, so that Ambrose can write about "the birth of Christ from the virgin, or the spread of the Church," for not only Christ but the Church too was contained in Mary's womb, as he says in his commentary on the canticle: "From the womb of Mary was brought into the world the heap of wheat surrounded by lilies [i.e., the faithful], when Christ was born from her" (5:2). For Christ is inseparable from His Church; hence when Mary gave birth to Him, she at the same time gave birth to the Church.

This, however, does not place her above the Church, as is pointed out by St. Augustine, who elaborates still further the relation between Mary and the Church. "Mary is a part of the Church, a holy member, an excellent member, yet but a member of the whole body. If of the whole body, surely more is the body than the member." Nevertheless, he too assigns a certain "mystical," or rather "typical" (in the specialized exegetical sense of certain persons or things being "types" of others), meaning to her motherhood in relation to the Church. "Consider how the Church obviously, is the bride of Christ; and, what is more difficult to understand, yet true, how she is the Mother of Christ. The Virgin Mary preceded her as her type. Whence, I ask you, is Mary the Mother of Christ, if not because she gave birth to the members of Christ? I hear the voice of your heart: Mother Church. This mother is holy, honoured, similar to Mary; she brings forth, yet is a virgin."

Here again we have the typical relation between Mary and the Church, based chiefly on the fact of the virginal fecundity of both. As the virgin mother of Christ gave birth to Him, and with Him to the Church, so the virgin Mother is inseparable from the Church. St. Augustine states that it is by the love of Mary that men come to baptism and become members of Christ. It is this ancient Latin teaching that was echoed by the Second Vatican Council when it decided to incorporate its Marian doctrine in the Constitution on the Church.

A few years ago (1964), at the parish church of Castel Gandolfo, Pope Paul spoke of Mary in these terms: "We must not separate devotion to Mary from that which have to pay her divine Son . . . It would otherwise be like wanting to look at a lamp without paying any attention to the light that it brings." He continued: "The lamp is beautiful if it has light and Mary's light is Christ, whom she bore and generated for us." Such too is my own thought in writing of Mary *in relation to Christ and the Church.* I see her, venerate her and love her precisely because of her Son. Love of Mary is the surest way of growing in the love of Christ.

Pope Paul establishes that Catholic devotion to Mary is solidly based, that it is built on the one true foundation; "for other foundation no man can lay, but that which is laid; which is Christ Jesus" (I Cor. 3:11). Mary was called to cooperate with God in the economy of salvation on a higher level than that of any other agent, as becomes clear when we contrast her role with that of St. Joseph as a case in point. His place in the mystery of the Incarnation is indicated in the gospel: "Joseph, the husband of Mary, of whom was born Jesus who is called the Christ" (Matt. 1:16). Joseph was chosen in the divine council to be the guardian and protector of the Child and His mother. Like us in all things save sin, Christ entered life through a human family and experienced the dependence on the care of others that is the condition of every human child. Joseph's responsibility was great, and in some way he was the representative and the special instrument of Divine Providence. He belongs to the order of the Incarnation and for that reason is immensely honored by the Church. His appointment as the patron of the universal Church would seem an appropriate reward for his unique services. But at the same time his connection with the Incarnation and still more with the Redemption cannot be compared with that of Mary; it was on an essentially lower and more extrinsic scale. The Mother and the Child are indissolubly joined in the eternal plan; they were joined in the promise made to our first parents; they were joined in the fulfillment of the Incarnation;

and consequently they should be joined in every stage of the Redemption.

The relevance to other Christians of the solemn pronouncement on the Virgin Mary is clear and decisive. It is an authoritative refutation of the charge of a false Mariology that Catholic devotion to Mary is uncritical and indefensible. Those who accept the Christian revelation must admit that the devotion to Mary in the Church rests on her unique relations with the Redeemer, as revealed in Sacred Scripture. To dispose once and for all of a misconception of a fundamental truth should surely be a great step in the direction of Christian reunion. The fears of those who felt that chapter 8 would be seen as a gratuitous affirmation of Mariolatry likely to repel seekers after unity were seen to be quite groundless.

But for Catholics too chapter 8 has a deep ecumenical significance. To theologians it will be a stimulus for a new study of the mystery of the Incarnation. The widespread interest in the place of Mary in this mystery, as witnessed by the number of Marian congresses and current theological studies, indicates that the Church has its eyes fixed on her and is reading more deeply into this fundamental mystery by studying the Church in Mary. "It is not only that Mariology can profit from ecclesiology," says Karl Rahner, "that a full-scale theology of the Church, from within which Mary can be assigned her place in the being and functioning of the Church, can be of great service to Mariology and safeguard it against sentimental distortions and subjective isolation. The reverse possibility has just such a meaning; Mariology fertilizes ecclesiology."

The true attitude toward Mary's honor had been well expressed in a recent study on her part in Redemption. "The sole cause and arbiter of Our Lady's privileges is God. It is not what *we* think but what He thinks and freely decrees that determines the dispositions of grace; and that divine decree we can know through revelation and through revelation alone."

"For behold all generations shall call me blessed." Each generation will add its own tribute to Mary's greatness.

Through the centuries of the Church's existence the slender "Tower of Ivory" has become a great complex structure. But it has been erected on the foundation of Jesus Christ.

Mary is proposed as "type and image" of the entire Church because she was so closely associated with Jesus in the divine plan of salvation. This association must be understood, however, in the light of the basic fact that Jesus Christ is the one mediator between God and man. Hence any aid, mediation, or association in spreading the work of salvation flows from, and is dependent on, the all-sufficient and superabundant redemptive work of the divine Saviour Himself.

Cardinal Suenens of Belgium affirmed the dignity of Mary in these terms—

> Mary is not the Mother of some man who just happened to become priest, redeemer and savior of the world. She is not like the mother of an army leader who, as a mother, is in no way intimately associated with her son's victory. Because God freely willed it, Mary in her subordinate role associated fully in the mystery of Christ in the ever-loving Church, she both cooperated in the redemption perfectly accomplished by the Son. Mary is not some kind of an instrument to be tossed aside after she has fulfilled her duty of generation. Rather her physical motherhood is extended in a spiritual one. Mary exercises a real influence, a steady action of inspiration in the mystical body of Christ.

He then compared the motherhood of Mary and that of the Church—

> The motherhood of the Blessed Virgin Mary is a type and an example of the Church's motherhood; there is, therefore, a very close connection between Mary's motherhood and the preaching of the Gospel to the world. It is the task of theologians to express that connection in proper terminology, but it should be brought to light." [Sept. 17, 1964.]

The Council made its own the doctrine taught as long ago as St. Ambrose (d. 397) that Mary is the "type" of the Church in faith, hope, and charity and perfect union with Christ. To understand this, it may help to think of Mary, virgin and mother, as the example who always precedes the Church. This can be worked out from her faith and obedience at the Annunciation, her perfect holiness toward which the Church is still striving (see Eph. 5:27), her entry in depth into the mystery of salvation which the Church ever seeks to penetrate, the example of her self-sacrificing motherly love, and her assumption, body and soul, into heaven in which she simply goes before her.

After the three irenically phrased paragraphs describing Mary's maternal role in the life of the Church, the document then deals with a more particular theological question: the relation of the Church to Mary as to her type.

Pope John XXIII had spoken of Mary as Mother of the Church in terms of the love of the faithful for her. It is another reference to the twofold motherhood of which he often spoke.

"We, however, by the grace of God, honor Mary as the mother of Jesus and the mother of the Catholic Church. She receives not only the homage of exquisite art, which testifies to her in every place, but the ever fervent, beautiful, and profound veneration felt for one who never for a moment fails in her motherly care.

"Let us always share in the sorrows of Mary when we see her beside the cross of Jesus. Let us pour out our hearts to her in the saddest moments of our life, remembering her first."

The doctrinal commission of the Council stated that the title Mother of the Church was implicitly contained in the Constitution on the Church but decided not to use it. John had approved the title himself even before he became pope; his discourse excluded the main objection, that it would set Mary outside the Church, for he declared her part of it. Some conjectured that he wanted to win over the minority who were troubled at the sobriety of the Constitution. Others said that he sought to avoid wounding Protestant confidence, by adding nothing new doctrinally and by showing Mary's relation to her Son. The title itself is outside the Constitution, though the document surely implies it and logically leads to it. Mary is both a member of the Mystical Body and the mother of that body: "She holds the loftiest position in the Church after Christ, and the nearest to us."

Pope Paul saw in the title Mother of the Church the means of integrating Mary into the Church while at the same time showing her exalted position. As Cardinal Montini he had already advocated this formula when he intervened in the debate of December 5, 1962. Giving his support to Cardinal Suenens (Dec. 4), he declared: "I approve that the Blessed Virgin be honored as Mother of the Church." Since then he made increasing use of the title—on August 15, November 14, and December 4, 1963, and May 27, October 11, and November 18, 1964.

Pope Paul affirmed his emphasis on the role of Mary as Mother of the Church—

> Should we not be glad that we have been led to this authoritative, beautiful correct statement of the ecumenical council, through the wise inclusion of the chapter on the Blessed Virgin Mary in the monumental Constitution on the Chuch? Should we not give to her the title *Mother of the Church,* which we have recognized as due to most holy Mary at this precise moment of the development of the doctrine of the Church, of the meaning of salvation-history? The mysteries of the life of Christ were inseparably linked and shared by his holy Mother. The union of Christ and his Church, cannot be separated from her who is the Mother of the Incarnate Word and whom Jesus Christ himself wanted so near to himself in the mystery of our salvation.

The Pope expressed his own feelings on Mary as type of the Church on May 27, 1964, to a general audience in St. Peter's Basilica—

> Whosoever will want to meditate on these two names: "Mary and the Church" will find most beautiful reasons for associating the two terms in a lively admiration for the design of God who desired human cooperation, that of Mary, that of the Church, in the fulfillment of the Redemption. He will find in the age-old tradition of theology and the liturgy frequent references to Mary and the Church in the same symbols.
>
> He will find that Mary is the ideal figure of the Church, *Ecclesiae typus,* the model of the Church, as St. Ambrose says [in Lc.

II, 7]; she, as St. Augustine afterwards writes, "who mirrors in herself the image of Holy Church."

We can say more: in Mary, full of grace, we find all the riches which the Church represents, possesses and dispenses. Above all, in Mary we have the virginal Mother of Christ and in the Church we have the virginal Mother of Christians, one a natural maternity, the other a mystical one.

St. Augustine further says, "Mary engendered physically the Head of the Mystical Body and the Church engenders spiritually the limbs of that Head who is Christ" (*de Sancta Virg.*, 2).

Not only can we contemplate in Mary the figure of the Church, but we can discover many other relations that show how the election of Mary is connected with that of humanity redeemed. It would be sufficient to recall the presence of the Madonna in the Cenacle on the day of Pentecost in order to admire how that day, which was for Mary a new and terminal fullness of grace, was for the Church the initial moment of the effusion of grace, almost the birth of the life of the Holy Spirit.

"Thus also under this title, Our Lady can be considered and honored as the Mother of Holy Church, which is also marked by the very sweet and very exalted title of mother, Mother Church: the prerogatives of the Virgin communicate themselves to the Church. Mary possesses and has in herself to an eminent and perfect degree all the perfections and graces with which Christ endows His Church."

In Mary the whole mystery of the Church was already present in the world, heralding the other form of its perfect presence in the world which we commonly call the Church. Mary was, then, the fulfillment of the history behind her, the reality to which all the earlier "types" pointed; and she was also herself the perfect "type" of the ecclesiastical mystery to be revealed and given to the world in its other and later form at Pentecost. That is why Mary is called the "prototype" or "prime-symbol" of the Church.

On this occasion of the proclamation of Mary as Mother

of the Church, November, 1964, Pope Paul concluded his address with a prayer to her under this title, referring to the various members of the Body of Christ—

O Virgin Mary, Mother of the Church, to you we recommend the entire Church and our Ecumenical Council!

You, *"auxilium Episcoporum,"* aid of bishops protect and assist the bishops in their apostolic mission, and all those priests, religious and laymen, who help them in their arduous work.

You, who were presented by your Son Himself, at the moment of His redeeming death, as Mother to His best-loved disciple, remember the Christian people who entrust themselves to you.

Remember all you sons; support their prayers to God, preserve their faith, strengthen their hope, increase their charity.

Remember those who are in tribulation, in need, in danger and particularly those who suffer persecution and who are in prison because of their faith. For those, O Virgin, obtain fortitude and hasten the desired day of just freedom.

Look with benign eyes on our separate brothers and condescend to unite us, you who brought forth Christ as a bridge of unity between God and men.

O temple of light without shadow and without blemish, intercede with your only Son, mediator of our reconciliation with the Father [cf. Rom. 5:11] that He may have mercy on our shortcomings and may dispel any differences between us, giving us the joy of loving.

To your Immaculate Heart, O Mary, we finally recommend the entire human race. Lead it to the knowledge of the sole and true Saviour, Jesus Christ; protect it from the scourges provoked by sin, give to the entire world peace in truth, in justice, in liberty and in love.

And let the entire Church, by celebrating this great ecumenical assembly, raise to the God of mercy the majestic hymn of praise and thanksgiving, the hymn of joy and exultation, because the Lord has worked great things through you, O clement, O pious, O sweet Virgin Mary.

St. Germanus of Constantinople referred to Mary's role in guiding the Church in peace and tranquility—

By your most acceptable prayers, strong with the authority of Motherhood, to our Lord and God, creator of all, your Son who was born of you without a father, steer that ship which is the

Church and bring it to a quiet harbor . . . Crown with the triumph
of victory this your city, which has you both as a tower and a
foundation and keep the House of God, surrounding it with strength
and preserve always the beauty of the temple . . . Stretch out to
the whole world your helping hand . . .

St. Jerome in the office for the feast of the Immaculate
Conception stated—

It was fitting that fullness of grace should be poured into that
Virgin who gave glory to the heavens and the Lord to the earth,
who has brought peace to the earth, who has given faith to the
gentiles, who has overcome sin and given law to life, who has
made the crooked ways straight.

Pope John liked to point to Mary as the mother to be
esteemed and imitated by her children. She is the model and
type of what her children should aspire to be—

As the Saviour's Mother, the Virgin Mary shared intimately in the
work of redemption by which Christ made us members of himself
and called us to "become children of God" [John 1:12]. Like a
mother who always wants the best of everything for her own children
she leads us, by her admirable example and powerful intercession,
towards the perfection of love. In her body she is the Mother of
Christ, and she is spiritually the Mother of his mystical body which
is the Church so she is truly the Mother of God and our Mother
too.

Whatever may be the conditions of our life and our responsi-
bilities, we are all unfolded in the motherly embrace of the Virgin
Mary, who does for us what every mother does so lovingly for
her own children: she loves us, watches over us, protects and inter-
cedes for us. To reward her show yourselves always faithful Catholics in your love to the Virgin Mary, "the holy Mother of all the
members of Christ's Body" [Pius XII, *Myst. Corp.*]. All Catholics
are therefore Our Lady's children and their love for Mary obliges
them to reflect upon their common membership of the family of
God's children, and to share in the customary expressions of the
devotion which the Church of Jesus Christ has, for so many centuries felt for the Saviour's Mother.

Dear children, avoid everything which savors of singularity
and instead look for the traditional Marian devotions, handed
down to us from the beginning through all the succeeding genera-

tions of Christians, both of the East and the West. Such a devotion
to the most holy Virgin is the mark of the truly Catholic heart.

The Marian movement among Catholics of recent centuries is considered one of the advances of the post-Reformation Church. It would be a cruel and incorrect misrepresentation to attempt to explain this movement as essentially a reaction again Protestantism's attitude to Mary. For one thing,
this movement is a continuation from the late patristic period,
and it was recognizably gathering strength during the Middle
Ages.

The Marian movement is the work of the Holy Spirit, the
unfailing source of the Church's life. But since its most notable
development took place during the centuries of the counter
Reformation, it inevitably reflects the temper and spirit of this
era in the Church's history. The Marian movement marched
from wave to wave guided by the Church's magisterium; it
brought to the Church a deeper appreciation of Mary's privileges and dignity. The accent that this movement put on Mary's
unique privileges, associated with and seen as the natural consequences of her dignity as the Mother of God, seemed to
suggest that she was conceived first and foremost as *set apart
from the rest of the Church.* As a consequence theological
study concerning her became more and more dissociated from
the theological study of the other mysteries of God, with the
exception of Christ the Redeemer. Christ is the term of theological comparison that the parallel thinkers within this tradition love to dwell upon, Christ is divine in dignity—Mary's
dignity arises from her divine motherhood; Christ redeemed
the world—Mary, in all things a perfect mother, cooperated,
so far as was possible to a creature, in the work of redemption; Christ rose in glory—Mary is assumed to reign in glory.
United on earth in the mystery of salvation, they are now
united in heaven.

But as a theological movement the Marian movement was
in some respects very much circumscribed. Its primary impulse
lay in the Church's instinctive faith in Mary's greatness. Its

principal sources were the pronouncements of the Church's magisterium in the last century. I have already remarked that this theology became more and more isolated from the rest of theological reflection. As I have said, the schema on Our Lady first proposed to the Council for discussion acknowledged that it has not made great use of the usual theological sources—Sacred Scripture and the tradition of the Church. But this theological tradition had shown itself notably reluctant to acknowledge and make use of a most venerable Christian tradition, of both Eastern and Western churches, emphasizing not the contrast between Mary and the rest of the Church, but her role *at the very center of the Church's mystery,* as its supreme embodiment and the type of its perfection. One might well ask, Why had the modern theology of Our Lady, indefatigable in its labors to unfold the riches of revelation with respect to Mary, neglected until very recently this clearly recognizable tradition? Perhaps we may give this answer: This tradition, as we find it, for instance, in the great Latin Fathers such as Ambrose and Augustine, has immediately concerned itself not so much with Mary's greatness as with the mystery of the humble and hidden presence of that greatness in the world. But this line of thought had little appeal for the post-Reformation mentality.

On the one hand, this mentality conceived the Church's presence in the world after the manner of a military conquest. It found it difficult to contemplate the Church's mission in terms of humility and self-effacement; on the other hand, the Marian movement has given itself the task of enumerating the glories of Mary, and failed to recognize the theological importance of her self-effacing presence in the world as the type of the Church, of her humility and service as well as of her faith and obedience.

It is not difficult to see, however, that the new mentality, which has had such an influence on the course of the Council, which feels that metaphors of triumph do *not* express the demeanor which the Church should adopt in its encounter with the modern world, and which strives to understand in its wholeness the mystery of the Church's presence in this world, is profoundly attracted by the inspiring vision of Mary, in whom the mystery of the Church finds its supreme fulfillment, even when she is hidden in the midst of the world, and whom the Church must study if it is to come to know itself.

As Mary is united to her Son, she holds a special place in the Church. Otto Semmelroth, S.J., says, "The Church discovers and rediscovers her own features in Mary's countenance." Karl Rahner, S.J., declares, "The Church advances over the dark roads of time and the centuries as long ago Mary went up from Nazareth to Bethlehem, carrying within her the eternal Word."

Father Alexis Kniazeff makes this observation on Mary's motherhood: ". . . it is exercised within the Church and not above it . . . Mary herself is part of the Church and cannot be set over against the Church, even in the aspect of her spiritual motherhood . . . it does not place her above the Church. It could be thought of as a gift with which Mary entered the Church and which would make her a mother *in* the Church, not of it." (*Faith and Unity,* May 1966, p. 58.)

Here I should like to devote a few thoughts to Mary and the Church, suggested by the gospel of St. John.

After the mention of Mary at the foot of the cross the fourth gospel says nothing else about her. We know from the Acts of the Apostles that she was among the apostles when after a long and intense preparation in prayer, they received the Holy Spirit. Through this we see the link that on the one hand united Mary to the Spirit—she who conceived through Him—and on the other, to the Church whose mother she is.

According to his custom, John invites us to consider these realities not in precise circumstances, which he has not related, but in a spiritual way. John's Gospel is the Gospel of the Holy Spirit. It is also an ecclesiastical gospel, in the very measure in which the data he proposes are those with which the Church will be constituted and which will give it the power to live and develop: faith and the sacraments.

We may surely ask, Did not the long and profound influence of Mary on John, of Mary the first in faith and in whom the Church saw its beginnings, play a decisive role in St. John's vision of spiritual realities, and the manner in which he presented them in his gospel?

When the rivers of living water began to flow from the side of the Crucified, who was actually there to receive this effusion if not the Virgin Mary? But these rivers of living water are inseparable from the blood, that blood which Jesus received from His mother. Now tradition has seen in this water and blood the symbol of the Spirit and the new birth, of Baptism and the Eucharist, the symbol of the Church being born from the side of Christ.

Between Mary and the Church there exists much more than a comparison. Mary is the first link in that line of life that the Mystical Body of Christ will form through the centuries. But this link resembles no other, for it is she who gave Christ His body, and at the cross the entire Church is to be found concentrated and assembled in her—that Church whose foundations are to be strengthened a few days hence in the Cenacle and over whose cradle Mary will bend with maternal solicitude.

The Holy Spirit is to be found in her, as the origin of the Mystical Body of the Church as well as of its Head, of Christians as well as of Christ. Thus we cannot reduce her maternity simply to the affective order. Her role is effective. She does not have as her mission only the duty of adopting us as her children and of forming Christ in us; she must work also to build up the Church in us now in the Spirit, without whom our birth to the divine life and our position as children of God would not be realized. She is not just the mother of individual Christians but the mother of the Christian community, the Church.

These realities remain more or less implicit in the gospel, and we would ask ourselves if they really express the evangelist's mind. He has explicitly pointed them out in the Apocalypse. There in fact the role of the Virgin is described under the traits of woman: "Clothed with the sun, and the moon was under her feet, and upon her head was a crown of twelve stars. And being with child, she cried out in her travail and was in anguish of delivery." (12:1-2.) Mary struggles against the dragon who is ready to devour the child as soon as it is delivered. But while the child is raised up to God and to the throne, the woman receives the two wings of the great eagle to fly into the desert. And the dragon was angered with the woman, and went away to wage war with the rest of her off-spring, who keep the commandments of God, and hold fast to the testimony of Jesus. (12:17.)

Mary furnishes the Church with a perfect model for the children she must bring into the world over the centuries. The Church will conquer with Mary, through the blood of the Lamb, and like Mary the Church will be a mother by remaining united to Jesus, source of divine life.

In the Apocalypse, Mary appears as having arrived at the place destined for her and been reunited to her Child. In the gospel she is before all else the one who accompanies the Church in its march here below. It is under these two aspects that she must be considered. Triumphant in heaven, whose queen she is, sharing the glory of her Son, she remains nevertheless occupied with her children on earth. Mary continues to recognize their need, and she obtains it for them through her intercessory prayers. She never ceases to bring them forth to the life of heaven and guide them to her Son. "Do whatever he tells you" (2:5).

It is because Mary is the type of the Church that Jesus commits her to the beloved disciple and him to her. The period of Mary's human motherhood in regard to the Son of God incarnate, the fulfillment of which Christ had already declared at Cana, here finds its completion: she, the Mother of God, becomes the type of Mother Church. Henceforth it is not possible to speak of the Church, of its humility, motherliness, faith, or joy, without conceiving of Mary, the mother of the Lord, as the pure expression and first realization of the Church.

Karl Rahner has written of Mary's role in the Church—

The mission to praise the grace of God as something which has come and conquered contains the obligation of the Church to call herself the one who is holy throughout the ages, and to make this statement about herself in a concrete way as seen in the prize of the saints given by name. The Church must therefore begin with Mary, the Protomartyr and the Apostles; but she cannot stop there. She must retain the power which was active in the primitive Church when she "canonized" Our Lady, the Protomartyr and the Apostles, otherwise she would simply have been the holy Church at one time without *being* it still; she could no longer actually praise the grace of God which has really been granted to her as something which saves and sanctifies. [*Theol. Invest.,* III, 96-97]

The Church is not the community of Christians who are already recognized as predestined for salvation and who can be isolated as such. She is therefore the Church of sinners, of those who are *in via,* the Church of hope, of the secret of election kept concealed by God and of the impossibility of anticipating the judgment here on earth. Since, however, she must be the city set on a hill and the assembled flock of Christ—in other words, the visible Church—the validity of the office cannot be dependent in the individual case on the inner holiness of the office-holder. This truth in its turn, however, must not be allowed to cancel out the other truth, viz., that the Church is meant to be and to appear as the community of eschatalogical salvation and of victorious grace. Hence, at the decisive points of the history of salvation, i.e., for example and above all in Mary, the historical salvific function and the holiness have fused separately into one." [*Ibid.,* p. 104]

In his book *Mary, Mother of the Lord,* Father Rahner points out that in our theology we must consider man as well as God because the Word became man. And if we speak of Christ, then we must also treat of His mother, through whom He became man. Rahner seems to say that the fundamental concept of Marian theology is that Mary is the most perfect expression of Christianity. Mary is the perfect Christian because she received God into her body and mind and heart and served in the salvation of all men. "Mary is the perfect Christian, the Christian human being exemplified as such, because in the faith of her spirit, and in her blessed womb, with body and soul, then, and all the powers of her being, she received the eternal Word of the Father" (pp. 36-37).

Moreover, if perfect Christianity means the unselfish service of others, Mary is the most perfect because she conceived the salvation of all men by her consent in faith to the divine plan and by her motherhood of the Saviour. The People of God are the Church in pilgrimage. We speak of holy Mother Church as we speak of holy Mary. It is not possible to speak of the Church, of its motherly character, of its faith or its joy, without conceiving of Mary, the Mother of the Lord, as the pure expression, the archetype and the firmest realization, of the Church. Thus we say "Mary and the Church, the Church and Mary (*Maria-Ecclesia, Ecclesia-Maria*)."

Martin Luther saw Mary in her function as a representative of the Church, and he considered her also a spiritual mother within the Church, by reason of her intimate communion with Jesus, her Son. These assertions, often quite poetic, must not be detached from the context of the preaching in which they occur. The coherence of Luther's thought shows that he gave a real place to Mary in his faith and piety and that he had the family conception of the Church which we noted in the New Testament. He discovered in Mary a spiritual mother in the Church: "Mary is his true mother, Christ is his brother and God is his Father."

Mary, therefore, according to Luther, appears clearly as the type of the Church, our mother. She helps us to think of this motherhood of the Church in her ministry. When we think of the ministry of the Church, we must think of Mary as the type if we would understand her spiritual motherhood. The Church is the Bride of Christ: "He loved her and gave himself up for her, that he might sanctify her, having cleansed her by the washing of water with the Word, that he might present the Church to himself with splendour, without spot or wrinkle or any such thing, that she might be holy and without blemish . . . ; he nourishes and cherishes her" (Eph. 5:25-32). And St. Paul added to this conjugal description of the Church: "This is a great mystery, and I take it to mean Christ and the Church." If, for St. Paul, the conjugal union of the Christian and his wife is a symbolic sign, a mystery, which directs our spirit toward the reality of the love of Christ for the Church, His bride, then, for St. John, the motherhood of Mary in regard to Jesus and to the Beloved Disciple, a brother of Jesus, is a symbolic sign, a mystery, which directs our minds to the reality of the love for us of the Church our mother. The mystery of Mary is also of great import; it is applied to the Church, the mother of the faithful who are the brethren of Christ.

As Brother Max Thurian observes: "The necessary authority of the Church must be expressed according to the motherly love of the Church, and Mary, the type of the motherly Church, is able to teach the ministers of the Church, the authority in the Church, and all the faithful, that only he who has a strong motherly concern for spiritual direction, without fancifulness, can truly express the love of the Father which gives rise to faith, nourishes, consoles and heals by His Word and by the signs of His Presence."

It is proper to apply to specific Marian devotions a teaching that is contained in the Council's Constitution on the Sacred Liturgy. Though insisting that the liturgy far surpasses any popular devotion, this document says: "Popular devotions of the Christian people are warmly commended, provided they accord with the laws and norms of the Church. Such is especially the case with devotions called for by the Apostolic See . . . Nevertheless, these devotions should be so drawn up that they harmonize with the liturgical seasons, accord with the sacred liturgy, are in some fashion derived from it, and lead the people to it." (Art. 13.)

Devotion by its very nature is spontaneous and unpredictable. The Council obviously hoped to effect some changes in Marian devoton, but it did not attempt to legislate them. It warned against distortions and excesses and trusted that the faithful would take these warnings to heart. It did not ask for any diminution of devotion to Mary; on the contrary, it urged that such devotion become universal and unceasing.

Pope Paul VI stressed the role of Mary as the model and type of follower of Christ. She is the perfect witness of the Son of her love and the Son of God—

Her virtues, her earthly experiences as told us in the gospels give her to us as our exemplar. It is enough to look at but a few of the events which the gospels record of the Mother of Jesus; and for this we do not need a magnifying glass—only the exacting lens of Christian piety . . . let us strive to approach this perfect model given to us for our own everyday living. Even those who assume a worldly attitude often feel a longing for an ideal beauty; this happens especially when the idols we took for masterpieces turn out to be miserable phantasms. Newspapers, books, literature, the theater are full of them. It is then that we must lift up our eyes, as Christians have always done, and look for the Madonna to draw from her the lessons we need.

Mary is a model to be loved and imitated—

She is our Mother and our teacher. If in all the events of life, we look at once to Mary, we can hear the inspiration: be Good, be patient and charitable, act in this manner, suffer cheerfully and present your pains to the Lord as I also have done. Always hope; always love; give to your life the real meaning of dedication to Christ—and thus you will receive salvation. These are elementary lessons but no one can choose to ignore them." [Aug. 15, 1968]

Or in the words of Roger Schutz of the Taize community, Mary would be the harbinger of humility and simplicity in the Church. It should be "more and more as being first the Church of the humble, the oppressed, the hungry. In effect, the Virgin Mary could proclaim that, by the coming of Christ, the humble would be elevated and the powerful humbled."

This truth places Marian devotion in a light not new, of course, but different from the light in which most of us have been used to viewing it. If Christians would make the imitation of Mary the foundation of their devotion to her, it would constitute a radical change in Marian devotion, and would bring great advancement to individuals and to the Church. Imitation of Mary would lead men to practice that charity for which the world cries out so desperately.

In keeping with the thought of Mary's apostolic role in the life of the Church we have this statement from the Decree on the Apostolate of the Laity from Vatican II—

The perfect example of this type of spiritual and apostolic life is the most Blessed Virgin Mary, Queen of the Apostles. While leading on earth a life common to all men, one filled with family concerns and labors, she was always intimately united with her Son and cooperated in the work of the Savior in a manner altogether special. Now that she has been taken into heaven "with her maternal charity she cares for these brothers of her Son who are still on their earthly pilgrimage and are surrounded by dangers and difficulties; she will care until they are led into their blessed fatherland." All should devoutly venerate her and commend their life and their apostolate to her. (No. 4)

René Laurentin makes this the following assessment of the role of Mary in the Church. She is the summation of the life of Christ communicated and expressed; so is the Church—

In short, the Church which is essentially Jesus Christ spread abroad and communicated, implies two modes of participating in Jesus Christ. It acts *in his name* and lives with his life. It brings down the divine gifts from heaven and receives them. It exteriorizes God's action by performing sacramental rites, and it interiorizes it by faith. It administers the means of grace and causes them to bear fruit. Its first aspect is that of being the official representative of Christ; it is summed up in Peter and his successors. Its second aspect is mystical communication with Christ; this is summed up in Mary. So we are led to make the following distinction: insofar as the Church is an external society, earthly and hierarchical, with the office of visibly taking the place of Jesus Christ between his two comings, the idea of it develops apart from mariology; but insofar as it is an inward society, heavenly and spiritual, with the office of holding invisible communion with Christ, it has its perfect realization in Mary." [*Op. cit.*, p. 131]

On the Feast of the Assumption, 1968, Pope Paul spoke of the relation of Mary and the Church—

The Madonna was both Mother and Virgin. The Church is also a Mother who brings forth all of us—not by human power but by the gift of the Holy Spirit; we might say by a virginity of service. Again we might consider in what way the Church is united to Christ. It must be just as Our Lady was united to Him. She, the all-holy Virgin, had but one ideal, one love, one plan: during her whole life she was interested only in offering her homage to God;

she was absorbed in consecrating herself immeasurably to Jesus; the Church likewise, has no other purpose, no other end than that of bringing Christ to the world . . . the Holy Virgin from her place in heaven, near the Heart of the Saviour, pours out on us the light of her example.

Later in the same address he declared—

What the Church does in every man, Our Lady has done in her Son. Thus we call her Mother of the Church because she gave birth to us in the supernatural order in the same way in which she brought forth Christ the Lord into being.

4

DEVOTION TO THE BLESSED VIRGIN IN THE CHURCH (66-68)

66. Mary was involved in the mysteries of Christ. As the most holy mother of God she was, after her Son, exalted by divine grace above all angels and men. Hence the Church appropriately honors her with special reverence. Indeed, from most ancient times the Blessed Virgin has been venerated under the title of "God-bearer." In all perils and needs, the faithful have fled prayerfully to her protection. Especially after the Counsil of Ephesus the cult of the People of God toward Mary wonderfully increased in veneration and love, in invocation and imitation, according to her own prophetic words: "All generations shall call me blessed; because He who is mighty has done great things for me" [Luke 1:48-49].

As it has always existed in the Church, this cult is altogether special. Still, it differs essentially from the cult of adoration which is offered to the Incarnate Word, as well as to the Father and Holy Spirit.

Yet devotion to Mary is most favorable to this supreme cult. The Church has endorsed many forms of piety toward the Mother of God, provided that they were within the limits of sound and orthodox doctrines. These forms have varied according to the circumstances of time and place and have reflected the diversity of native characteristics and temperament among the faithful. While honoring Christ's Mother, these devotions cause her Son to be rightly known, loved and glorified, and all His commands observed. Through Him all things have their being [cf. Col. 1:15-16], and in Him "it has pleased [the eternal Father] that all his fulness should dwell" [Col. 1:19].

67. The most holy Synod deliberately teaches this Catholic

doctrine. At the same time it admonishes all the sons of the Church that the cult, especially the liturgical cult, of the Blessed Virgin, be generously fostered. It charges that practices and exercises of devotion toward her be treasured as recommended by the teaching authority of the Church in the course of centuries, and that those decrees issued in earlier times regarding the veneration of image of Christ, the Blessed Virgin, and the saints, be religiously observed.[1]

But this synod earnestly exhorts theologians and preachers of the divine word that in treating of the unique dignity of the Mother of God, they carefully and equally avoid the falsity of exaggeration on the one hand, and the excess of narrowmindedness on the other.[2] Pursuing the study of sacred scripture, the holy Fathers, the doctors, and liturgies of the Church, and under the guidance of the Church's teaching authority, let them rightly explain the offices and privileges of the Blessed Virgin which are always related to Christ, the source of all truth, sanctity, and piety.

Let them painstakingly guard against any word or deed which could lead separated brethren or anyone else into error regarding the true doctrine of the Church. Let the faithful remember moreover that true devotion consists neither in fruitless and passing emotion, nor in a certain vain credulity. Rather, it proceeds from true faith, by which we are led to know excellence of the Mother of God, and are moved to a filial love toward our Mother and to the imitation of her virtues.

The last major division of chapter 8 deals with the way in which the Church venerates Mary. The Council commends a generous devotion to her which is at the same time Christ-centered and free from all exaggerations. Here as elsewhere the Council in its choice of language and emphasis tries to avoid anything that might unnecessarily offend the sensibilities of our separated brethren. After pointing out that this cult, though very special, that is, higher than that of all the saints, is essentially different from the worship due to the Incarnate Word, to the Father and to the Holy Spirit, the Con-

---

[1] *Council of Nicaea II in 787: Mansi,* 13, 378-89 (*Denz.* 302 (600-601); *Council of Trent, Session 25: Mansi,* 33, 171-72.

[2] Cf. Pius XII, radio message, Oct. 24, 1945: *AAS,* 46 (1954), p. 679, and the same Pontiff's encyclical *Ad Caeli Reginam,* Oct. 11, 1954: *AAS,* 46 (1954), p. 637.

stitution speaks of "many forms of piety toward the Mother of God, provided that they were within the limits of sound and orthodox doctrines . . . according to the circumstances of time and place and have reflected the diversity of native characteristics and temperament among the faithful."

This is a short section of just two articles but a most important one. The prayer life of the Church must be based on sound theology. The ancient axiom holds here: *Lex orandi, lex credendi,* "The law of prayer is the law of belief." We must never forget the centrality of Christ, nor must we forget the place of Mary in the plan of salvation. As the late Archbishop Paul Hallinan of Atlanta said—

> If our Lord Jesus Christ is kept in the center of the Christian life of prayer and worship, all the other elements appear in their proper place. Surely the place of His Mother Mary was made clear by Christ himself at the wedding feast of Cana, and at Calvary by Mary herself and should be clear to all of us. Because she is the Mother of Christ she has a claim upon our filial love and proper veneration. But to attempt to center our religion in Mary, to exaggerate her cult, to multiply her devotions in such a way that Christ is obscured or forgotten would be a blasphemy to the Son, and an embarrassment to the memory of the Mother, and a pathetic deviation on the part of those baptized in Christ.

Devotion to Mary has always been one of the hallmarks of the genuine Catholic life, and it is essential for its authentic development that a proper devotion to her be instilled in our people. But there is a difference between the liturgy and private devotions. The liturgy is the public expression of the Church's worship; it is a special source of grace and of instruction. Private prayer and devotions are not a substitute for the liturgy, nor does the liturgy supplant the need for private prayer; both forms must have a place in the Christian life.

In Marian devotion a distinction is made between the liturgical honor accorded Mary, such as the various feast days in the Church's calendar and the prayers of the Mass for each day, and the private form of prayer. Principal non-liturgical devotions would be the devotion of the rosary—in the Western

Church and in the litany of Loretto. Often such form of devotion is public, but distinct from the liturgy as the official honor of the Church. It may be noted that some Marian festivals are very ancient, such as that of the Annunciation and of the Assumption, while others are of recent origin, for example the Feast of Our Lady of Lourdes and of the Immaculate Heart of Mary. The celebration of feast days may be limited, such as that of the Immaculate Conception, which is not a holy day of obligation throughout the whole Church. Other feasts may be proper to a religious community or to a nation or locality, such as Our Lady of Guadalupe (Dec. 12), though there is a tendency at the present time to suppress such feasts, particularly if they seem to duplicate a festival already celebrated by the universal Church.

In his first encyclical, *Ecclesiam suam* (Aug. 6, 1964), Pope Paul noted the importance of devotion to Mary. It was surely not his first statement about the Blessed Virgin, but it has singular value because of the document. Mary

> reflects this vision most perfectly and wonderfully in herself; she lived it on earth and now in heaven she rejoices in its glory and beatitude. Devotion to Mary is happily flourishing in the Church today; and we . . . gladly turn our thoughts to her to admire in her, Mother of God (and therefore also Mother of us) the model of Christian perfection, the mirror of true virtue, the pride of humanity.
>
> We regard devotion to Mary as a source of gospel teaching. In our pilgrimage to the Holy Land we wished to learn the lesson of real Christianity from her, the most blessed, lovable, humble and immaculate creature, whose privilege it was to give to the Word of God human flesh in its pristine and innocent beauty. To her now we turn our imploring gaze as to a loving mistress of life, while we discuss with you, the spiritual and moral regeneration of the life of the Church.

Mary's role in the mystery of Christ and of the Church calls for an acknowledgement and response which we call veneration. The contemplation of Mary is a sound help to the proper understanding of Christ and His work. The special cult of the Virgin Mary is based on her exaltation by God's grace and her presence in the mysteries of Christ. That cult is always relative, that is, it is always directed beyond Mary herself. She must be shown greater honor than the saints and angels, but it is an honor that is essentially on the same plane as hers, being different only in degree. But the honor paid to the three Persons in God is adoration due to Him alone. Devotion to Mary is possible only because she refers us to the Lord and because in her God reaches out to men—God to Whom alone a man can give himself completely. In order that the Son my be adored the Church seeks for sound devotion to the Blessed Virgin. The Council points out that devotion may vary according to time and place. It would be unrealistic to judge the Marian devotions of other ages by what is customary at the present time or the Marian piety of other nations by our own particular taste.

Calling for renewed devotion to Mary, the Council warns against two extremes. In matters of faith and piety there is no place for snobbery and narrow-mindedness, though they may wear the mask of practicality. But exaggeration must also be avoided. There have been some strange examples of it in the course of centuries, even in our own day and in our own nation, which do harm to the Church and are a scandal to our Christian brethren. Devotion must be nourished at the sources of our faith—Scripture, the interpretation of the fathers and doctors of the Church, and the liturgy. Private revelations are not to be considered sources of the faith, and the Council warns against vain credulity. Honor is due to Mary as the Mother of God and the Mother of men.

Pope John XXIII has made this personal, poignant appeal for devotion to Mary as a need for all Christians. He felt it must not be put aside as unworthy of her or unnecessary for her children—

> Mary is with us, among us; she protects and helps us; she leads us along a sure road. More than once the Pope has heard the wistful cry of some souls—among those brothers of ours who, since the beginning of the sixteenth century have been cut off from the unity of the Church—who exclaim with profound sadness: Is it

possible not to love one's own mother? And yet some of them have managed to forget her altogether, or at least to keep her at a distance, as sometimes happens, alas! in certain families in which the mother when advanced in years is borne with as a burden instead of still being cherished with loving care.

In May, 1967, Pope Paul gave an address on the nature of devotion to the Blessed Virgin; he spoke of "our spirituality in regard to Our Lady most holy." He referred to Mary's faith and said that devotion to her must be "Christ-centered and Church-centered." I present these extracts from that exhortation—

> We believe that this is the only safe way, to promote our devotion, our spirituality in regard to Our Lady Most Holy. It is well known how this holy and blessed name of Mary has become today, in a certain sense, like that of Christ's, "a sign that shall be contradicted" [Luke 2, 34].
>
> There are those who exalt the devotion to Mary, at times in an excessive manner, and beyond the proper doctrinal and devotional limits which harmoniously merge Marian piety within the theological and liturgical framework proper to the Catholic Church.
> The Council enacted no laws concerning devotion to Mary, and indeed the Church has no such laws, except the obligation to attend Mass on certain Marian feasts—in this country, the Assumption and the Immaculate Conception. But the Council forcefully stated what is the mind of the Church concerning the faithful's devotion to Mary.
> This section surely urges the faithful to pray to Mary, "Mother of God and Mother of men" with persevering prayer. Indeed it is not just an exhortation to prayer in general but also specifically for unity, as we shall show later in the next chapter.
> The Council document recalls that "in all perils and needs, the faithful have fled prayerfully to her protection." It reminds us that devotion to Mary "differs essentially from the cult of adoration, which is offered to the Incarnate Word, as well as to the Father and Holy Spirit. Yet devotion to Mary is most favorable to this supreme cult."

On February 8, 1964, Pope Paul said:

We must never forget who Mary is in the eyes of God: "the fixed object of eternal design." . . . We must never forget who Mary is in the story of salvation: The Mother of Christ and thus the Mother of God, and through marvelous spiritual relationships, the Mother of believers and the redeemed, the *janua coeli*—"the gate of heaven." The panoramic vision of the theology which is centered around the humble *ancilla Domini*—"handmaid of the Lord" must never vanish from our spiritual sight if we wish to understand any of the true, authentic and exhilarating things which the privileged creature on whom the divine transcendence unfolds and settles and in whom the Word of God takes human reality . . . By honoring Mary one discovers her superlative function in the economic of salvation.

The Pope recalled the role of Mary in the mystery of salvation as portrayed by the liturgy—

Moreover, the liturgy deepens our understanding of Mary, model of the Church as Virgin and Mother. "By her belief and obedience . . . she brought forth on earth the very Son of the Father. . . ." [art. 63]. In the liturgy the Church receives the word of God in faith and obedience, becoming herself a mother, for the liturgy is at once the expression by the Church of her fidelity to Christ and actualization of her maternal life-giving role in regard to her children.

Saved and made spotless through the redemptive mystery of Christ, virginal in her fidelity to Christ in loving service and obedience, maternal in her loving care of Christ's own, Mary is the perfect model of all that the Church seeks to be. In the liturgy the Church deepens in herself that participation in the mystery of Christ which was perfectly realized in Mary. The Church becomes more like Mary in every liturgical celebration.

Our liturgical experience of the Church as virgin and mother enables us to grasp more fully the mystery of Mary, virgin and mother, and model of the Church as the Council envisions her. The Church is virginal, pure, and unstained, the spouse of Christ, but a mother who communicates life through the sacraments particularly and who guides and directs her children along the path of virtue to their destiny in heaven.

The ultimate motive [wrote the late Romano Guardini, noted German theologian] which leads the believer to Mary is, . . . the desire to be within the orbit of her holy life. He desires to dwell in her proximity, in the aura of her being and the intimacy of her mystery. The word "mystery" does not stand here for a riddle in the sense of something still unsolved. It conveys rather a quality, a potentiality, a sphere; the governance of God in man, the breath of eternal life. Here the worshipper wants to enter, here he wants to dwell, to breathe, to become quiet, and to receive comfort and strength to continue his life with renewed courage." [*Prayer in Practice*, p. 138]

It was not a happy hour, when people thought that for the sake of Christ's honor they had to minimize His intimate link with His mother. "This did not come about purely by accident. Man has a tendency to exaggerate that which he loves and in this way a good deal of exravagance, not to say fantasy, entered into his relation with Mary,. Add to this the influence of legend; the instinct of the people to invest the figures of those dear to them with extraordinary attributes and to fill their lives with miraculous events. Finally, there is a tendency towards sentimentality and mawkiness. All this was bound to lead to abuse in connection with the veneration of Mary. It is not surprising, therefore, that criticism of every kind, justified and unjustified, has arisen and that many serious minds have been unable to find a way to Mary. They have tried to disassociate themselves from exaggerations and obliquities, but, unable to distinguish the wheat from the chaff, they have thrown all away. This is a thousand pities because the history of Christian piety shows how well the true veneration of Mary accords with the most vivid conception of Christian truth. [*Ibid.*, p. 139]

Though the Church allows a large variety of devotions, and indeed desires "the cult, especially the liturgical cult, of the Blessed Virgin, to be generously fostered," the Constitution warns against false exaggerations as well as against a too narrow outlook. Theologians and preachers should be guided in the first place by Sacred Scripture, and then by the fathers of the Church, the doctors, and the liturgy, and realize that all the offices and privileges of the Blessed Virgin are "always related to Christ, the source of all truth, sanctity and piety."

There follows a special warning to the faithful against a merely superficial affection as well as against vain credulity, which is contrasted with "true faith by which . . . we are moved to a filial love towards our mother and to the imitation of her virtues." These warnings are not without serious foundation. No external devotion, however much approved by the

Church, can by itself ensure salvation; it must be accompanied by an inner attitude corresponding to the outward action. Credulity too, which—contrary to popular ideas—is a fault and is opposed to the virtue of faith, is sometimes connected with Marian devotion. This is too obvious in the avidity with which at times the most incredible visions and revelations are accepted and propagated by some Catholics, but without authorization, an attitude that can only bring the faith into disrepute.

Unlike some devotees of the past and of the present, the Church regards Mary not as a refuge for man in his mediocrity but as a beacon to guide him on the path to self-perfection. If this teaching could be made known to all and taken to heart, devotion to Mary, far from being downgraded, would be raised to a higher level of excellence and effectiveness than it has ever known before. It would put an end to the irrational exaggeration that marks the devotion of some and to the cynical aloofness that marks the non-devotion of others. For who is there whose faith, hope, and charity, whose humility and fidelity and patience, are so perfect that he has no need of a model in whom all these virtues shine forth in the highest degree?

As part of the renewal following Vatican II it is the intention of the Church to transform subjective Marian piety into an ecclesiastical Marian piety, that is, into participation in the structure or composition of the Church. The feasts of Mary should be directed to recognize and celebrate her unique role in the economy of salvation. As for ecumenism, this does not mean that Catholics should fear to mention Mary or the role that she enjoys according to Catholic teaching. Mary is a touchstone of Catholic truth.

In regard to the origin of Marian devotion in the first centuries of the Church, Pope Paul made this remark at the Mariological Congress held in Portugal in 1967: "With the study of all the monuments of Christian antiquity, the admirable harmony of praises given in every age to the Virgin Mother of God will be more clearly understood—a harmony unused in its beginnings but growing in clarity and sublimity as time went on so that now we hear 'as it were the voice of a great crowd, and as the voice of many waters, and the voice of mighty thunders' [Apoc. 19:6]."

Before Christmas, 1966, he spoke of the veneration of Mary within the context of the mystery of the Incarnation—

> The great event, the great mystery of the Incarnation, the birth of Our Lord Jesus Christ, twice begotten, as an inscription in the old Basilica of St. Peter read: "without mother in heaven, without father in earth, in other words, the eternal Son of God the Father and Son in the time of Mary, one in the divine Person of the Word that unites to His divinity the humanity of Jesus Man-God, our Saviour, our brother, the Supreme Priest between heaven and earth, the center of history and of the universe."
>
> This is the best liturgical season for the veneration of Mary. We should meditate on what the Council teaches us regarding the veneration we owe her, and we should allow our souls to be permeated with the fervor and poetry aroused and demanded by this veneration.

Devotion to the Mother of God, raised by grace to a position above all other creatures in relation to her Son, dates from ancient times. The first prayers were those of praise and intercession; the idea of imitation came at a later date. All prayer to her is a fulfillment of the words of the Magnificat: "All generations shall call me blessed" (Luke 1:48). The Council commends various liturgical forms of this piety and also approves devotions in accord with the liturgy. The effect of such veneration is that while honor is paid to the mother, the Son is duly recognized, loved, and glorified.

With typical tenderess Pope John spoke of genuine love for Mary—

> Whoever believes in our Lord Jesus Christ, whoever belongs to the holy Church has a Mother, Mary! Life is always unfolding: we leave our childhood behind and our youth, and we still pray, and even more frequently to our Mother in heaven. . . .

What marvelous offerings of faith can be seen in the whole Christian world! By the side of churches dedicated to Our Lord and inside them we find the presence and the memory of Our Lady. And this has been so ever since the miraculous event of our Redemption. The New Testament, we might say, begins with the words of the divine messenger: "The angel of the Lord announced to Mary." At the highest level of all communications between God and man is Jesus, the Redeemer of the world, who shortly before his death on the cross, entrusted Mary to His apostle John, saying to him: "Behold your Mother" and entrusted his disciple to Mary with the words: "Behold your Son."

Again, Pope John spoke of Mary as the Mother of all men, a title he was fond of using:

The Mother of Jesus, who is our Mother too—Oh how I love to associate these two titles!—is one of the richest sources of our consolation, the richest after Jesus, who is His very nature, light and life; she is rich in comfort and joy and encouragement for all the children of Eve, who have become her own children through the redemptive sacrifice and will of Christ.

This explains the whole world's devotion to the Virgin whom her saintly cousin Elizabeth truly hailed as "blessed," in reply to Mary's confession of humility in the *Magnificat,* which remains the everlasting canticle of mankind redeemed, the song of the past, present and future.

Typical of medieval penchant for titles and figures of speech through the centuries is this thought from Bernard, abbot of Clairvaux, once used for the feast of the Holy Name of Mary (Sept. 12)—

Let us cling to Mary's footsteps, my brethren, and cast ourselves at her blessed feet with earnest supplication. Let us hold her and not let her go, until she blesses us, for she is mighty. For as the fleece is between the dew and the threshing-floor and the woman is between the sun and the moon, so is Mary between Christ and the Church. But perhaps you marvel not so much at the fleece covered with dew as at the woman clothed with the sun. The juxtaposition of the sun and the woman would be wonderful; how much more than this intimate relationship?

How can a being so frail exist in such burning heat? Rightly do you wonder, holy Moses, and desire to gaze more closely. But put off the shoes from your feet, lay aside the clinging folds of worldly thoughts, if you desire to draw near.

Thus Mary has a place of special honor in Christian thought, and the praises for Judith the Hebrew heroine are often applied to her: "You are the glory of Jerusalem, you are the joy of Israel, you are the honor of our people" (Jth. 15: 10). Because of her share in the history of salvation Mary is indeed the glory, the joy, and the honor of the human race, and more particularly of the Jewish people, for out of all the nations Israel was chosen to give birth to the Redeemer. The Greek Christian writers, in addition to the title Theotokos, used many terms of praise for Mary: she is "The Holy Virgin," "The Immaculate Virgin" (Eustathius, fourth century), "Holy Mary," "Mistress," "Lady," and "Ever-Virgin"; and the Syrian St. Ephraim (d. 373) uses many phrases of her, including "Mediatrix of all the world" (in his prayer to the Mother of God, extant only in Greek).

Various nations have their favorite titles by which they honor Mary: as the Greeks call her Theotokos, so the English most often say "Our Lady"; the French say "Notre Dame," the Germans "Unsere Liebe Frau," and the Italians "La Madonna," while in America she is most often called "The Blessed Virgin."

The simple title "Saint Mary" was the most frequent dedication of a medieval English church. The title "Queen" has a long tradition in Latin (as in the prayer *Salve Regina*), and in 1954 the Feast of Our Lady was instituted under the title of Queen by Pope Pius XII.

How, for example, does the church now look upon the rosary? Pope John XXIII, the prime mover of the *aggornamento* in the Church, prayed the entire fifteen decades of the rosary every day for the last several years of his life; and he said in *The Diary of a Soul*: ". . . It has come to be an exercise of continuous meditation and of tranquil daily contemplation which keeps my spirit open to the vast fields of magistry and my ministry as chief pastor of the Church and universal Father of Souls."

Pope Paul VI sent a message and blessing to a million people attending the final session of Father Patrick Peyton's recent Family Rosary Crusade in Barcelona, Spain. And his nuncio, Archbishop Roberi, told the throng that the rosary "is like a summary of the Gospel, a breviary thereof, available to everyone, an intuitive teaching that goes to the depth of the soul." Pope Paul in his peace encyclical of September 15, 1966, devoted nearly half of the text to urging the faithful to recite the rosary during October to Our Lady, Queen of Peace.

The rosary is a kind of summary of Christian belief—a brief review of the mysteries of the life of Christ, for our meditation and imitation. It is a very simple prayer but also very profound. Pope Leo XIII was the great exponent of it in comparatively recent times, though more than fifty popes have urged its use by the faithful. Some Protestants too use the rosary as a help to prayer. Perhaps the large rosary rallies of the past have little place in Catholic life today; but it seems that this form of prayer will always have a special place in Catholic life and practice, even with a revision of Catholic devotional life.

Romano Guardini favors the rosary

> because we dwell on the person and life of our Lord within the context of the life of His Blessed Mother. We call to mind fifteen successive events—from the Annunciation to the Coronation of the Blessed Virgin in heaven—and dwell on the significance of these events, not so much as events in themselves, but as events related to, and experienced by, the one who of all people was closest to our Lord. [*Prayer in Practice*, p. 95]
>
> This prayer contains the ever-renewed appeal for the intercession of Mary which is capable of embracing all the sorrows that afflict human life. It includes meditation upon that God's filled existence and participation in and rejoicing over its riches. It brings also a restful abiding in her presence. At the same time it brings out the true significance of the figure of the Virgin, because the focus of all such meditation is the part which she played in the life of Christ. [*Ibid*, p. 138]

In discussing the rosary the Holy Father likened the role of the priest to that of Mary: "Mary gives Christ to humanity; the priest also gives Christ to humanity, but in a different way: Mary by means of the Incarnation and the effusion of grace with which God has filled her; the priesthood by means of the powers of sacred orders, the ministry that generates Christ in the flesh and afterwards communicates him through the mysterious ways of charity to souls called to salvation." He then quoted the famous lines of Cyril of Alexandria from the council of Ephesus: "Through you, O Mary, the apostles preached salvation to the people; through you the cross is adored and the devil is put to flight; through you the faithful have come to salvation." [Oct. 7, 1964.]

The role of shrines in the Catholic and Christian life seem to fullfill a human need. Thousands go in pilgrimage to Lourdes each year, not just to beg the intercession of Mary but to honor and praise her. Not only Catholics venerate Our Lady at such a sanctuary but Anglicans and Protestants, and even Jews and Moslems.

The chapter on the Blessed Virgin Mary says nothing of these shrines. It is clear that they are in disfavor with some people who consider pilgrimages outmoded. Yet Pope John made it one of the first acts of his papacy to visit four famous Italian shrines of Mary. Pope Paul, after the Council, sent the papal Golden Rose to the Shrine of Fatima, reviving a papal custom long out of use. In the accompanying message he said, "In this manner we intend to entrust to the care of this Heavenly Mother the entire human family with its problems and worries, with its lawful aspirations and ardent hopes." And not long afterward he sent another Golden Rose to the Shrine of Our Lady of Guadalupe, in Mexico. He authorized the crowning of the Statue of La Macarena, Our Lady's title as patroness of Seville, and sent a message praising the city's ancient devotion to Mary. In the course of his message he emphasized that a "true and deep Marian devotion must of necessity be reflected in a truly Christian life."

During his visit to India, Pope Paul visited the relatively

obscure shrine of Our Lady of Bandra. He would have visited the world-famous Shrine of Our Lady of Czestochowa in Poland, for the Polish Millennium of Christianity, if the Communist government had permitted him to come. As it was, he said Mass on the occasion in a chapel of Our Lady of Czestochowa in St. Peter's Basilica.

It is evident that popes, and therefore the Church, continue to recognize the positive spiritual value of Mary's traditional shrines, as a testimony of the pilgrims' faith and as centers of the living liturgy.

Pope Paul has often urged a renewal of the concept and devotion of the Virgin Mary according to the principles of the Vatican Council. In May, 1968, he declared: "The Virgin is not presented by the council as a solitary figure in an empty sky, but as a unique and most beautiful creature. Mary is honored with the high office and dignity of the Mother of God-made-man, and for this reason she is the beloved of the Father and the temple of the Holy Spirit. For this gift of grace Our Lady takes first place far ahead of all other creatures, earthly or heavenly. The Madonna is for Christ, near Him and with Him. We must not for an instant forget that she is the Mother of God and this justifies our veneration, love and faith." Mary is Mother of the Church now as she was in its early days, he said, and she is the example of all the fundamental Christian virtues, especially of faith and of obedience to the divine will.

As Archbishop of Milan the Holy Father sought to remind the faithful of the "pure goal" of Marian devotion—

The liturgy is not only a means of teaching us dogmatic truth; it is also a school of holiness, and one of the principal means of uniting our souls with Christ. Hence it is to be hoped that the work of this congress will be devoted especially to this aspect of Marian liturgy. This will, where necessary, bring devotion to the most blessed Virgin back to its pure goal, so that it recovers its real function in bringing souls to Jesus by the swiftest, most total and most loving transformation possible of the old man into the new man of righteousness and Christian holiness. Any other form of Marian piety, insufficiently orientated in this direction, would thereby necessarily show itself as deficient and as displeasing to the heavenly Mother.

The surest sign of love for Mary is the imitation of her virtues, especially of her faith, her love, and her union with Christ. While the practice of prayer to Mary, of asking her intercession, dates from the earliest Church, the idea of imitating Mary came later. But the imitation is surely a valid form of veneration and devotion, and we may here treat of that aspect of love for Our Lady. Pope Paul VI cited the words of St. Paul "therefore I beg you be imitators of me as I am of Christ" and stated that with even greater reason they may be applied to Mary. He stressed the point of following Mary's example in love of Jesus, since "the imitation of Christ is the regal way to be followed to attain sanctity and to reproduce within ourselves, according to our abilities, the absolute perfection of the heavenly Father." (May 13, 1967.)

He alluded to the practice of children's imitating the good qualities of their parents; Mary is the model for all her children: "In fact just as the teaching of parents becomes far more efficacious if they are strengthened by the example of a life conforming to the norms of human and Christian prudence . . . so the sublime virtues of the immaculate Mother of God attract souls in an irresistible way to the imitation of the divine model, Jesus Christ, of whom she was the most faithful image."

Mary is the exemplar of what Christians should be in the mystery of the Church, and it is necessary that the Christian life retain all the warmth and familiarity connected with motherhood. To neglect an accurate and realistic teaching about Mary deprives the Christian faithful of an ideal of the Christian life which they need for an integral development, an ideal provided by God as a guide to a truly personal relationship with Christ himself.

Cardinal Seunens of Belgium has phrased the imitation of Mary in terms of service to others—

It is not enough to honor Mary with some pious exercise. Rather, real authentic devotion demands an active service. The word *devotion* comes from the Latin *devovere* which implies dedication and collaboration. Marian piety is too often divorced from life and apostolic activity. I ask therefore that this connection be clearly shown so that Mary will not only be an example for our admiration but that faithful Christians will also be invited to associate themselves actively within her present spiritual motherhood in the service of men in today's world. [Sept. 17, 1964.]

Pope Paul emphasized the duty of redeemed humanity toward the Mother of Christ and of the Church—

We wish once more to call the attention of all sons of the Church to the indissoluble link between the spiritual motherhood of Mary . . . and the duties of redeemed men toward her, the Mother of the Church. She is the Mother of the Church, not only because she is the Mother of Christ and his closest associate in the new "economy" in which the Son of God took a human nature from her . . . but also because she shines forth to the whole community of the elect as a model of the virtues. [May 13, 1967.]

Cardinal Newman wrote of those who pour out their love for Mary in words not meant in any strict and absolute sense and perhaps never intended to be quoted but which have managed to get into print and are used against Marian devotion—

Of all passions love is the most unmanageable; nay more, I would not give much for that love which is never extravagant, which always observes the proprieties, and can move about in perfect taste, under all emergencies. What mother, what husband or wife, what young man or young woman in love, but says a thousand things foolish in the way of endearment, which the speaker would be sorry for strangers to hear; yet they are not on that account unwelcome to the persons to whom they are addressed. Sometimes, by bad luck, they are written down, sometimes they get into newspapers, and what might be even graceful, when it was fresh from the heart and interpreted by the voice and countenance, presents but a melancholy exhibition when served up cold for the public eye. So it is with devotional feelings. Burning thoughts and words are as open to criticism as they are beyond it. What is abstractly extravagant may in particular persons be becoming and beautiful and only fall under blame when it is found in others who imitate them. When it is formalized into meditations and exercises it is as repulsive as love-letters in a police-report.

Among the saints a special position belongs to the Blessed Virgin Mary. In its liturgy Orthodox reverence has her as the most exalted among God's creatures, "more honorable than the cherubim and incomparably more glorious than the seraphim." In Greek theology the distinction is very clearly marked: there is a special word, *latria,* reserved for the worship of God, while for the veneration of the Virgin entirely different terms are employed (*duleia, hyperduleia, proskynesis*). These distinctions are used also in the Western Church.

In the Orthodox liturgy and prayers Mary is mentioned often, and each time is usually given her full title: "Our All-Holy, immaculate, most blessed and glorified Lady, Mother of God and Ever-Virgin Mary." Three chief epithets are applied to Mary by the Orthodox Church: "Theotokos" (Mother of God), "Aeiparthenos" (Ever-Virgin), and "Panagia" (All-Holy). The first of these titles was assigned to her by the Third Ecumenical Council (Ephesus, 431), the second by the Fifth Ecumenical Council (Constantinople, 553). The title Panagia, though never a subject of dogmatic definition, is accepted and used by all Orthodox.

The title Theotokos, discussed earlier, provides the key to the Orthodox veneration of the Virgin. They honor Mary because she is the Mother of our God and venerate her because of her relation to Christ. Thus they hold that the reverence shown to Mary, far from eclipsing the honor of God, has exactly the opposite effect: the more they esteem Mary, the more vivid is their awareness of the majesty of her Son, for it is precisely on account of the Son that they venerate the mother.

The Orthodox hold that Mariology is simply an extension of Christology. The Fathers of the Council of Ephesus insisted on calling Mary Theotokos, not because they desired to glorify her as an end in herself, apart from her Son, but because only by honoring Mary could they safeguard a right doctrine of Christ's person. Anyone who thinks out the implications of the great phrase "The Word was made flesh" cannot but feel a certain awe of her who was chosen as the instrument of so surpassing a mystery.

But the Orthodox honor Mary, not only because she is Theotokos but because she is Panagia, All-Holy. Among all God's creatures she is the supreme example of synergy, or cooperation, between the purpose of the Deity and the free will of man. God, who always respects human liberty, did not wish to become incarnate without the free consent of His mother. He waited for her voluntary response: "Behold the handmaid of the Lord; be it unto me according to your word" (Luke 1:38). As Nicholas Cabasilas said: "The Incarnation was not only the work of the Father, of His Power and His Spirit . . . but it was also the work of the will and faith of the Virgin . . . Just as God became incarnate voluntarily, so He wished that His Mother should bear Him freely and with her full consent."

Lutherans would see the analogy between the Mother of God and the Church as nowhere better typified than in the Magnificat. In this usage the words of Our Lady are not just a quotation from Scripture; the sentiments of Mary are the prayer of the Bride of Christ, the Church. What the Mother of Jesus said of herself expresses the faith of the Church that is mother of all. When the People of God sing the Magnificat, every phrase is informed by Hannah's song (cf. I Sam. 2.1) and by the psalter. The Mary-Church parallel shown in the Apocalypse (12:1) receives liturgical sanction.

The Lutheran liturgy has prayers for the feasts of the Annunciation, the Visitation, and the Purification/Presentation. The tract for the Annunciation includes the opening verses of the Angelus: "The angel of the Lord came unto Mary and said, 'Hail thou that art highly favored, the Lord is with thee; blessed art thou among women." The collect for the Annunciation is the same medieval post-communion prayer for the feast that Catholics use with the Angelus. The alleluia verse for the Visitation includes what is part of the Catholic Ave Maria: "Blessed art Thou, O Mary, among women and blessed is the fruit of thy womb." The Lutheran hymnal contains many references to the Mother of God—for example, "with virgin honor pure," "the blessed main," "chosen virgin mild," "full of grace," and "undefiled virgin mother." This hymnal has also a metrical version of the Eastern Theotokon: "O higher than the cherubim, more glorious than the seraphim, lead their praises; thou bearer of the eternal Word, most gracious, magnify the Lord!" As a post-communion hymn they often sing the medieval composition "O Lord we praise Thee, bless thee and adore Thee," with stress on the *corpus verum*: "May Thy Body, Lord, born of Mary, that our sins and sorrows did carry and Thy blood for us plead in all trial, fear and need: Lord have mercy!"

No other reformer has written so much about the Virgin Mary as Luther. He always held Mary in high esteem, as appears from his numerous sermons preached on Marian feast days and at Christmas. Some of his hymns and his commentary on the Magnificat provide further evidence for his evangelico-Catholic Marian piety. On the wall in his study he always kept a crucifix and an image of the Virgin.

Luther composed the words for hymns for vernacular worship at Christmas, some of which are revised from ancient Latin office hymns.

> Jesus we must now laud and sing,
> The maiden Mary's son and King,
> Far as the blessed sun doth shine,
> And reach to earth's utmost line.
>
> The tender heart, house modest, low
> A temple of our God did grow;
> Whom not a man hath touched or known
> By God's word she with child is grown.
>
> The noble mother hath brought forth
> Whom Gabriel promised to the earth;

Him John did greet in joyous way,
While in his mother's womb he lay.

Praise, honor, thanks, to thee be said,
Christ Jesus, born of holy maid!
With God, Father and Holy Ghost,
Now and forever, ending not.

Luther, the reformer, wished that daily vespers be continued with the singing of the Magnificat, which he loved. His commentary on this canticle of the Virgin Mary provides us with the best single source for learning the nature of his Marian piety. In Luther's eyes Mary teaches us what the true trust and love and adoration of God is: "Mary's heart remains the same at all times; she lets God have His will with her and draws from it only a good comfort, joy and trust in God. Thus we too should do: that would be to sing a right Magnificat."

Both Catholics and Protestants should examine their devotion to Mary and evaluate it in relation to their own spiritual lives and to one another's. "What is imperative here," says Walter Burghart, S.J., "is understanding on four levels . . . (1) Catholics must understand why Protestants reject the Catholic vision and veneration of Mary. (2) Protestants must understand why Catholics see Mary and honor her as they do. (3) Catholics must re-examine their present position on Mary—mind and heart, theology and devotion,—to discover if, and to what extent, they have given Protestants cause of legitimate concern. (4) Protestants must re-examine their present position on Mary— mind and heart—theology and devotion, to discover if, and to what extent, that position does injustice to God and to His Christ." (Ward, *Documents of Dialogue* pp. 260-61.)

5

MARY,
A SIGN OF SURE HOPE
AND OF SOLACE
FOR GOD'S PEOPLE
IN PILGRIMAGE
(68-69)

68. In the bodily and spiritual glory which she possesses in heaven, the Mother of Jesus continues in this present world as the image and first flowering of the Church as she is to be perfected in the world to come. Likewise, Mary shines forth on earth, until the day of the Lord shall come [cf. II Peter 3:10], as a sign of sure hope and solace for the pilgrim people of God.

69. It gives great joy and comfort to this most Holy Synod that among the separated brethren, too, there are those who give due honor to the Mother of Our Lord and Savior. This is especially so among the Easterners, who with ardent emotion and devout mind concur in reverencing the Mother of God, ever virgin.

Let the entire body of the faithful pour forth perservering prayer to the Mother of God and mother of man. Let them implore that she who aided the beginnings of the Church by her prayers may now, exalted as she is in heaven above all the saints and angels, intercede with her Son in the fellowship of all the saints. May she do so until all the peoples of the human family, whether they are honored with the name of Christian or whether they still do not know their Savior, are happily gathered together in peace and harmony into the one People of God, for the glory of the Most Holy and undivided Trinity.

The final section is brief, consisting of only two articles. Some authors have judged that the title of this section is offensive to Protestants because it seems triumphalistic. But to look to Mary as the image of the Church in glory and expressing the destiny of all the members of Christ is a sign of hope and strength and consolation. Christ in glory is a sign of hope for us; Mary is a kind of secondary sign of what human nature aided by grace can attain to. To sustain the Church in its aspiration for heaven, what better sign can it have than Mary, who shared in the redemptive mystery of her Son and Saviour?

The document concludes with an expression of joy that many Christians are devoted to Mary. This is surely true of the Orthodox churches, among some Anglicans, some Lutherans, and to a lesser degree Methodists and Baptists. In 1967 an Ecumenical Society of the Blessed Virgin was established in England to promote unity among Christians. Its original members were Catholics, Orthodox, and Anglicans. Since then other Christians have joined the group. It is hoped that the movement may spread to other countries as well. The Moslems too have great esteem for Miriam, the Mother of Jesus.

Chapter 8 shows what Mary is by reason of the will of God, and not by the will of the Church. By this I mean that Mary holds a special role in the mystery of salvation as chosen by God; her exaltation comes primarily from Him and not from the Church. The Church honors what God has done, so that it is not a case of shifting plans and levels and somehow making the whole situation more acceptable to those who differ but rather of frankly acknowledging the role and function that God has established in Mary. The teaching of the Church makes explicit what God has done in Mary and through her; there can be a growth and development in the appreciation of Mary's role in salvation history and in the life of the Church. The Church seeks to unfold in depth and with greater precision what God has done to and in the handmaid of the Incarnation and the helpmate with Christ in the mystery of salvation. In heaven Mary continues to exercise her role of partnership with Christ in the saving work of salvation; she is the type of what the Church as a body and what the individual Christians are destined to be.

The exaltation and glorification of Mary is founded on the will and the plan of God, not only on the design of the Church. If the Church were primarily responsible, then it might well consent to putting Mary on a lower plane to serve the cause of ecumenism. Indeed, the Church itself is in a way dependent on Mary's role; it was through her that the Son of God took human flesh and united Himself with mankind, who stood in need of salvation. Without Mary, in the present dispensation of Divine Providence there would be no Church.

Some differences between Catholics and Protestants in regard to the Blessed Virgin stem from differing concepts of Mary's role in salvation history. For Catholics, Mary had and has a special part to play in the whole divine plan of salvation; she entered into the life of the Incarnate Word and His saving mission in a way beyond that of any apostle or saint; she was His associate, His partner in the divine plan, even though she too needed redemption. She is man's model of holiness; she is his intercessor in heaven.

Protestants in general stress Mary's faith but do not assign her any special role or privilege in salvation history. "Jesus does not intend to confer any privileged status on his mother nor to transfer to her anything whatever of his merits, his power or his holiness. Like each one of his hearers, Mary can only be she who believes; she can only be *at the side of the disciples, not at Jesus' side.* Now where do we see her associated like the Apostles with the ministry of the Lord or even committed to any ministry . . ." (H. Roux, quoted by Y.M. Congar in *Tradition and Traditions in the Church,* New York: Macmillan, 1964, p. 409.)

Another Swiss Protestant author, R. Mehl, takes issue with Brother Max Thurian of the Taize community, who had sought to show the presence of Mary with Jesus at important moments of gospel history—the visitation to Elizabeth, the feast at Cana, and the Crucifixion. But "this bond between Mary and Jesus is nothing more than the bond of faith, which does not imply any cooperation in the redemptive work."

When Jesus died, Mary's role in His life ended. She retired into the shadows.

> Henceforth Mary's testimony is ended just as that of John the Baptist ended with the baptism of Jesus. In the death of the Son of God lies the whole of God's work which is proclaimed by the Church through the ends of the earth throughout the ages. Mary has therefore nothing more to do but to step back into line with the great cloud of witnesses. In giving Mary his disciple as as son and Mary as a Mother to his disciple, Jesus demonstrates in a fundamental and definitive manner his own distinctive character; he and he alone, lifted up on the cross is the unique author of salvation of all these witnesses, including his mother, who can never be more than witnesses to the cross and in no way his partners, collaborators or co-redeemers! [Roux, p. 414.]

Some Protestants see Mary as a type of the Church, but poor, humble and completely dependent on Christ. They do not see her as a figure of the redeemed, or her role in salvation, her merit, her grace, her glory in heaven. These points seem to be the basic reasons why Mariology is a thorny ecumenical problem. Even the Mary-Eve parallel which they read in the Fathers does not have the same meaning for Protestants as for Catholics. As one theologian would put it: "There is no second Eve, there is only a second Adam" (Roux).

Karl Rahner, S.J., cites as pivotal the study of Mary to our faith: "Mariology is the point at which the totality of the doctrinal difference between the Evangelical Church and the Catholic Church discloses itself." The Danish Lutheran theologian Kristen Skysgaard asserts: "There is probably no place where the difference between the two understandings of Christianity becomes so plain as in their different conceptions of the Virgin Mary." Brother Thurian has called Mariology "the most agonizing problem in ecumenical thought" and stated that "the doctrine and the veneration of Mary in the Roman Church create extreme difficulties." And once more: "One can see no

way through the problem posed by Mariology and the veneration of the Blessed Virgin in the Catholic Church."

Jaroslav Pelikan, a famous Lutheran theologian in
America, has commented—

> Neither the doctrine of the Church nor the doctrine of Christ
> can be fully articulated without some doctrine of Mary . . .
> Christological orthodoxy . . . was bound up with the clarification of
> the role of Mary in the plan of God. Protestant theology must ask
> itself whether this connection between Christiology and Mariology
> was a historical coincidence or whether there was in fact some
> ineluctable obligation in the orthodox confession of Jesus Christ
> that compelled the Church to speak as it did of His Mother.

Any criticism of Roman Catholic doctrine on Mary, he
says, "must be accompanied by a positive discussion of the
Mother of the Lord from biblical and evangelical perspective."
Mary cannot be ignored, because she "is a warrant of the
Christian declaration that our Lord was a true man, flesh of
our flesh and bone of our bone." She has significance for the
Church: ". . . the brief description of her career in the New
Testament is a summary of the Church's life in its elations and
in its depressions."

In the decree on ecumenism the Council fathers recognize
the difference between the churches on the subject of Mary,
but they also point out that such differences may point to
even deeper differences. "We are indeed aware that . . . views
are held considerably different from the doctrine of the Catholic Church even concerning Christ, God's Word made flesh,
and the work of the redemption and thus concerning the
ministry of the Church and the role of Mary in the work of
salvation" (art. 16).

There are differences of belief as to the nature of the Incarnation and the Redemption, the character of man's salvation, and the function of the Church in leading man to heaven.
If so, then the concept of Mary will also differ by reason of
her relation to Christ and to the Church He founded.

OUR LADY AND UNITY

Chapter 8 of *Lumen gentium* is considered the foundation upon which Catholic teaching on the Blessed Virgin should be based and orientated. From this point of view I wish to consider the thoughts and judgments of our brethren in other churches. And I like to think of a title for the Blessed Virgin used by Pope Paul VI which has special importance today, for the time in which we live, and for Christian unity.

All during his pontificate Pope Paul has stressed this role of the Virgin Mother in regard to unity. His words have often illustrated the connection between Christian unity and devotion to Mary. We may refer to several incidents in connection with the jubilee of Fatima in 1967. Prior to his journey, on May 10 at the usual Wednesday audience in St. Peter's Basilica, he said: "It is consolating to see how many Christian brothers, still divided from us, look with greater serenity and objectivity at the Catholic doctrine of the Madonna. It is no longer for them 'the Catholic heresy,' even if for them the Marian dogma still constitutes one of the major obstacles to union in the holy faith with the Catholic Church."

He spoke many times about Our Lady and unity, for example at Mass on October 11, 1963, on the anniversary of the opening of the Vatican Council. He delivered a homily during the liturgy offered in the Basilica of St. Mary Major (the center of liturgical devotion to Mary in the West). In addition to his allocution he expressed this fervent prayer: "O Mary, we pray to you for our Christian brothers still separated from our Catholic family. See how a glorious group of them celebrates your cult with fidelity and love. . . . Call all these sons of yours in the same unity, under your maternal and celestial protection.

"Your sweet, most human voice, O most beautiful among virgins, O most worthy among mothers, O blessed among women, calls upon this world to turn its glance towards the light which is the light of men—to you, who are the supporting light of Christ, the only and highest light in the world."

Pope Paul has often spoken of Mary and unity in regard to the Ecumenical Council. "While we turn in ardent prayer to the Virgin Mary that she may bless the Ecumenical Council and the entire Church, hastening the hour of the union of all Christians, our glance opens on the endless horizons of the whole world." And he concluded his prayer to Our Lady with a plea for unity: "Look with benign eyes on our brethren and condescend to unite us, you who brought forth Christ as a bridge of unity between God and man."

During the Unity Octave (Jan. 18–25) the Holy Father usually writes or speaks about Christian unity. At the noonday Angelus on the Sunday within this period of prayer he referred to Mary and her role in unity. In January, 1964, after his famous visit to the Holy Land he exhorted the crowd gathered in St. Peter's Square—

Today we must direct our prayer principally to the great aim of the reunion of Christians in the unity of the Church. You know that we are now in the Octave which is dedicated precisely to this great and noble end. And we will do so in the memory of our encounter with the ecumenical patriarch of Constantinople, which took place on the day of the Epiphany, imploring from the Lord that the great hope which was born on that day might be fulfilled. Certainly it will be necessary to have much patience, much understanding, no hurry; but the desire is great, and prayer will animate it even more. What is more, our Lady most holy, whom we implore as the Mother of Unity and the Mother of the Church, will favor it with her powerful intercession until it has been fully received.

Furthermore, we extend this, our desire for Christian Unity, also to the other great families separated from the Church, to those who are of the various Protestant denominations. Let us pray with fervor and determination, with great trust in Mary most holy.

In 1965, the Pope declared—

We must be united with Christ and for Christ. Any other unity would be fragile and equivocal. We must seek and promote unity among ourselves, among Catholics in the Church, in all forms in which human life is expressed; and unity with our separated brethren. We will send this great message to those brothers of ours and we will ask Our Lady to favor this unity, invoking her with the title *Mater Unitatis*, Mother of Unity.

This title goes back at least to the time of St. Augustine (d. 430), so that it is more than fifteen centuries old. But it is an idea as old as the Church, derived from Mary's union with Jesus and with the Church. Pope Paul VI referred to Our Lady and unity in his message to the Marian Congress in the Dominican Republic: "May the study and piety of Catholics concerning the Mother of God, have in addition to others, the merit of gathering around Mary, *Mother of Unity,* not only Catholics already in many different ways filially united to her, but also Christians still separate from us" (Mar., 1965).

Love of Mary was also a noteworthy part of the life of Pope John XXIII. I refer to it here because he had such an effect on the world for Christian unity and because he was deeply devoted to Mary. Shortly before his death, on June 3, 1963, he prayed to Our Lady and he prayed for unity. He urged devotion to her among the faithful during the Unity Octave of January 18–25 as bishop, as patriarch of Venice, and as pope. "May holy Mary, our loving Mother—who is so venerated among the eastern Christians and is waiting for the Christians of northern Europe to turn to her, she who never forgets anyone may she bless and watch over this Unity Octave."

The prayer of Jesus for unity would be fulfilled through the intercession of Our Lady. "In answer to the prayer of Jesus that all his brothers should be united among themselves and with him as he is united with the Father, the promise of one fold under the pastoral care of one shepherd will surely be fulfilled; let the attainment of this unity for which all believers in Christ are longing begin here, in the land of Lebanon, through you intercession, O Mary" (Oct., 1954).

When he crowned an image of Our Lady, he offered this hopeful prayer: ". . . may this image and all others which represent you in Italy, in the Near East and in the vast lands of Russia, inspire our prayers for this return to unity, which will be the joy and exultation of continents and seas, of earth and heaven, to Christ Jesus, your Son and our Brother, to whom in our emotion we dedicate the prayers of our lips and the throbbing of our grateful and joyous hearts, in the glorification of his blessed Mother and ours."

While I share the optimism of the Holy Father that devotion to Mary can foster Christian unity, I am aware that not all Christians consider love for Mary a means of promoting Christian unity. Some saw in the Pope's visit to Fatima an obstacle to ecumenical progress. The German Lutheran Bishop Deitzfelbinger said that the pilgrimage placed a "heavy burden on the ecumenical dialogue." He said that the best view to take of the visit was that it was directed to move men to pray for world peace. But for the Reformation churches, he added, only Christ is the "true Prince of Peace. The union of Christians lies not on the way to Fatima." Indeed, for the churches of the Reformation, it would not be easy to overcome "this new obstacle on the way of ecumenical dialogue."

Dr. Stanley I. Stuber, a Baptist and an observer at Vatican II, was also critical of the Pope's visit. He declared that "Protestantism does not venerate the Virgin Mary because on scriptural grounds it accepts Mary, not as the 'Mother of God,' but as the human mother of Christ. . . . Protestants are at an absolute loss when it comes to appreciating the Roman Catholic attitude in regard to the Virgin Mary. He thinks that Protestants consider the apparitions and miracles as verging on superstitution." But not all Protestants hold to this position: some of them visit shrines, pray the rosary, and honor Our Lady according to their own sentiments. They find the words of the New Testament a stimulus to their devotion.

At the Fifth International Marian Congress at Lisbon, held in August, 1967, to commemorate the fiftieth anniversary of the apparition of Our Lady at Fatima, several Protestants and Orthodox took part. Father Paul Melada, O.F.M., secretary of the Congress, said that it was "really the first time that a mutual dialogue has taken place" at such a congress. "From this contact between Catholics and their Christian brethren a more intimate understanding was born."

Father Charles Balic, O.F.M., president of the International Marian Academy, emphasized the ecumenical aspects of the meeting. Dr. Peter Meinhold, dean of the theological faculty of Kiel University, Germany, observed that the meeting was permeated with "mutual confidence" and a "spirit of communion."

Brother Roger Schutz, prior of Taize, expressed the wish that "our Catholic brothers never place the Virgin Mary in a position contrary to her proper attitude of humility and service." Brother Laurent of this community suggested that Catholics, Protestants, and Orthodox should be less steadfast in their Marian positions and asked that Christians break through this "circle of opposition" in regard to veneration of Our Lady. He stressed the "biblical humility" of Mary and said that no image of Mary should be shown without an image of Christ and that the names of God and Christ should be used first in all Marian prayers.

Besides the message from the Pope there was a letter from the Anglican prelate Archbishop Michael Ramsey of Canterbury, another from Athenagoras of Istanbul, patriarch of the Greek Orthodox Church, and another from Archbishop Germain, patriarch of the Serbian Orthodox Church. The last-named joined in praising the congress for its emphasis on the Blessed Virgin and the ecumenical tone which had been established, though he noted "that in the past the Church leaders had not always acted in accord with their Christian vocation, and had allowed themselves to be dominated by what was human rather than by what was divine."

ANGLICANS

Commenting on certain points of the Council that bear on the ecumenical task, Archbishop Michael Ramsey of Canterbury said that great as the role of the Blessed Virgin Mary was, "it is the role of one who is a creature, and a role which, filled with celestial glory, is always a reflection of and never a substitute for the unique glory of Christ the Divine Son. This is not to say that the Constitution of the Church has removed the great difficulty which we Anglicans feel about the Marian doctrines, but it is significant that it sets the doctrines in a context which checks the extremes of Mariological development."

Later, in his message to the Mariological Congress in Fatima of August 2–9, 1967, Archbishop Ramsey made this appraisal of devotion to Mary from the Anglican viewpoint (not shared by all Anglicans) —

> In the Anglican communion the role of the Blessed Virgin Mary is remembered daily in the use of the Magnificat in the daily office and we endorse the teaching of Holy Scripture: "All generations shall call me blessed." In the communion of saints we join our prayers and praises to those of the blessed saints in heaven.
>
> While we give honor to the Blessed Virgin who is truly described in the ancient writings as Theotokos, we have, as Anglicans, never accepted the dogmas concerning Our Lady which were defined in 1954 and in 1950 [the Immaculate Conception and the Assumption].
>
> We believe that it is unhelpful to Christian Unity when these dogmas are treated as *de fide* and as important as the Incarnation itself. We believe that these dogmas hinder rather than help the giving of due honor to the Blessed Virgin. Always we emphasize that the glory of Mary is but a reflection of the unique glory of her divine Son. From the beginning she points to Him in the words: "My soul doth magnify the Lord and my spirit hath rejoiced in God my Saviour."

Anglican theologian Dr. E. L. Mascall saw in the congress a strong sign of ecumenical hope because he found it "notable for its scriptural emphasis and for its refusal to isolate Mariology from the main corpus of Christian doctrine. So the Holy Synod has decided to expound both her relation to the Incarnate Word and the Mystical Body and also the duties of redeemed men towards her." Commenting on the Council's advice to theologians to walk the middle road between "exaggeration" and "niggling meanness," Mascall recalls also its warning: "Both words and practices which might give rise to misunderstanding on the part of the separated brethren or others are to be avoided." He regards as striking the "complete absence of the more questionable Mariological emphasis which a few years ago seemed to have got the upper hand."

Some years before, in the *Church Times* of August 18, 1950, the Anglican archbishops of Canterbury and York had taken exception to the then proposed definition of the doctrine of the Assumption. "There is not the smallest evidence in the scripture," they stated, "or in the teaching of the early Church of belief in the doctrine of her bodily assumption. The Church of England refused to regard as requisite for saving faith any doctrine or opinions which are not *plainly* contained in the scriptures."

It should be added, however, that the expected difficulties did not materialize, at least not as intensely as had been predicted. We should not gloss over or ignore difficulties that arise, real or imagined, but these should be taken in stride and not magnified out of proportion.

Bishop John Moorman of Ripon, England, also expressed his opinion about the title Mother of the Church—

At the end of the Third Session, in 1964, Pope Paul conferred upon Mary a new title when he called her "Mother of the Church." This was something of a shock and a disappointment, not only to the observers but to many of the fathers, who feared that it would undo something of what they had so carefully done in their statement on Our Lady. It looked as if, after all, the Pope was going to override the wishes of the Council and declare a new dogma. But this was not so. The designation "Mother of the Church" is not a new dogma, it is only a title and, surely, not one to which great exception can be taken. It can, for example, be argued that if the Church is the Body of Christ, and if Mary gave Christ his body, then it can reasonably be said that Mary is the Mother of the Church. Or we may link it with Christ's last words to Mary and and John at the Cross: "Woman, behold thy son. Son, behold thy mother," and say with Dr. Lightfoot: "Mary, the Lord's physical mother, now becomes, at the Lord's bidding and as a result of His work, the spiritual mother of all those who are to be born in Him." If the Church is the fellowship of those "reborn in Christ"—as the Evangelicals say—then there is a proper sense in which Mary can be called the Mother of the Church. [*Vatican Observed*]

After analyzing the decisive vote of October 29, 1963, on Mary's role in the Church, the Bishop stated: "Now that the Roman Church has done so much to try to 'contain' its Mariology, it is to be hoped that non-Roman Churches may be encouraged to take another look at their teaching on this important subject. In the past the tendency has been to be negative or to ignore the matter altogether." But this is not good enough. When the Anglican Prayer Book was finally settled in 1662, its calendar included five feasts of our Lord, two of red-letter status (Annunciation and Purification) and three of lesser solemnity (Conception, Nativity, and Visitation). In the previous century the Church had been more cautious. There was much superstition in England in the later Middle Ages, and the reformers, while anxious to retain a sound theology about Our Lady, were determined to purge the country of an excessive and unbiblical popular devotion. Their policy succeeded, for in the seventeenth century, while there was no flamboyant Mariolatry, there was some sound Mariology, as, for example, that expressed in Thomas Kent's hymn "Her Virgin-eyes saw God Incarnate born." The Tractarians also, and their successors, naturally adopted a certain amount of Roman Catholic phraseology both in their teaching and in their worship. But there still exists a certain amount of suspicion and confusion in Anglican thought. As I once heard a preacher say: "You know, the trouble is that you all think that Our Lady was a Roman Catholic."

He said that "the excesses of Rome have certainly led to neglect elsewhere, and this should be remedied. What we need is a positive and theological approach to the subject, to forget about the grottoes and processions, the visions and the fables, the sickly statuettes and the 'seven swords stuck in her heart,'

and try to see the place of Mary in the divine plan of man's
redemption."

As another Episcopalian theologian we may select John
Macquarrie of Union Theological Seminary, New York City,
who expresses a deep appreciation of Mary's role in the life
of Christ and the work of the Church and defends the title
Mother of the Church. Before commenting on that point, we
may consider some general concepts about Our Lady—

> Let me at once acknowledge that Mariology is a more peripheral
> theme in Christian theology than the doctrines that were discussed
> . . . though when the matter was first mentioned it was pointed out
> that Mariology should be discussed either in relation to Christology
> or in relation to ecclesiology—and Christology and ecclesiology are
> themselves closely related.
>
> However, even if Mariology is not central, there is no reason
> for omitting it. While we are trying to expound the Christian faith
> with reasonable economy and without getting lost in a morass of
> detail, we also want to expound the faith in its fullness, and it
> seems to me that a study of the Blessed Virgin does make a definite
> contribution toward understanding the Church and its relation to
> Christ. Finally, there may be some who think that here I am in-
> troducing a needlessly controversial and diversive topic. . . . If the
> divisions of Christendom are to be overcome, it can only be through
> frank discussion of such issues, not by evasion. A distinguished
> Protestant theologian, Max Thurian, who has recently written a
> book on this theme of Mariology, says: "Instead of being a cause
> of division amongst us, Christian reflection on the role of the Virgin
> Mary should be a cause of rejoicing and a source of prayer. . . . It
> is both theologically essential and spiritually profitable to consider
> the vocation of Mary with some freedom."
>
> How then is the Blessed Virgin presented to us in these incidents
> or mysteries that are related in the gospels? It seems to me that the
> best clue to the interpretation of her place in the New Testament
> teaching is afforded by the title "Mother of the Church." It was
> partly for this reason that we deferred a consideration of Mary's
> place in theology until we came to the doctrine of the Church.
> "Mother of the Church" is the title which Pope Paul VI proclaimed
> as appropriate to the Blessed Virgin when he adjourned the Vatican
> Council in 1964, and I believe that this particular title, more than
> any other, provides an interpretation of Mary's place on which
> Roman Catholics, Orthodox, Anglicans, and Protestants could
> agree.

The title has a firm scriptural basis. St. John's Gospel tells that the dying Jesus commended his mother to the care of the beloved disciple with the words, "Woman, behold your son . . . Behold your mother." In this gospel, which is above all theological and in which incidents are narrated only for their theological interest, it is surely highly probable that the words, "Behold your mother!" are addressed to the whole Christian community.

This points to the significance of Mary's role in the mystery of Calvary. Her presence is to teach the whole Christian community the importance of living the cross in daily life. Something must also be said about Mary's station at the cross. Again, when we remember the theological character of the Fourth Gospel, we should not suppose that this incident, moving though it is, has been included in the narrative just to heighten the dramatic effect. Rather, it is the parable of perfect unity and conformity with Christ, of the most complete identification and participation with him in his passion. We have already seen that through such participation or "dying with" Christ, the cross becomes intelligible as a saving act that brings wholeness. What closer participation is imaginable than that portrayed in the Fourth Gospel's picture of Mary at the cross? Kierkegaard has some very perceptive remarks about Mary's relation to Christ's suffering. He claims that Mary's own suffering is not to be understood as only a natural grief at the sight of Jesus' death, but as a sharing in his self-emptying, as if Mary were experiencing something of what Christ expressed in his cry of dereliction; and Mary's suffering is experienced in turn by every disciple who knows "the complete emptying of the human element in the face of God." So here again Mary appears as the prototype of the life of the Church, which must share in the suffering of Christ and must indeed finally give up itself altogether as a distinct association if it is to be resurrected and transfigured into the kingdom of God.

Berdyaev is completely correct when he affirms that reverence for the Blessed Virgin "is essentially distinct from pagan worship of the female principle." The practical benefits or, as has sometimes happened, abuses, which reverence for Mary has brought, cannot be determinative of her place in Christian thought and devotion. This has to be considered in theological terms, that is to say, in the light of Christology, ecclesiology, and the transformed anthropology that goes with them, as we have tried to show. If we have consistently held throughout this book that theological thinking must be rooted in the existential dimension of faith, we have maintained equally that practical attitudes have to be correlated with theological reflection and, where necessary, corrected to it. It seems to me, however, that it is precisely a renewed theological consideration of the issues involved that will increasingly lead Protestants (as it has led

some of them already) to abandon their negative attitudes toward
Mary, and to join with their Catholic brethren (and with the New
Testament) in a glad *Ave Maria!*

Even if many Christians should find that praying an Ave
Maria is a grave difficulty, I hope that they will admit Mary's
place in the plan of salvation as special and extraordinary and
that their fellow Christians' veneration of the mother of Jesus
should at least be tolerated if not imitated. Much growth in
sympathy and understanding is demanded of all Christians of
every persuasion to heal the wounds of disunity. This is as
true of Marian doctrine and devotion as in any other area of
Christian thought and practice.

After the international Mariological Congress at Lisbon
and Fatima during August 2–9, 1967, the *Christian Century*
carried three articles on devotion to Our Lady. The first one,
"Fatima: Reflections after the Fact," by Carmen Irizarry, a
Catholic, was a rejection of the veneration of Mary at this
shrine. She wrote that the apostolic letter of the Holy Father
"has set back the pastoral life of the Church many years, and
his appeal to the separated brethren in the name of Mary can
in no way contribute to the cause of ecumenism . . . the
political and dogmatic fall-out of the Marian rally in Portugal
has only begun."

By contrast, Dr. Paul Jewett of Fuller Theological Seminary, Pasadena, California, asked, "Can we learn from Mariology?" He suggests that Protestants might find some food for
productive thought in Mariology. He pointed out that "it may
be that Protestants should stand a little closer to Catholics"
and "that we have something to learn from them even in the unlikely locus of Mariology. After all, if their theology of the Virgin is too high, maybe ours is too low if indeed we have any
theology of Mary at all." He asks that Protestants reconsider
the judgments of Catholic scholars in regard to the usual
Catholic teaching about Mary, such as virgin birth and spiritual motherhood. He also suggests that consideration be given
to the possibility of Mary's assumption. "Even if we grant that

Our Lord's resurrection was not solitary and isolated, but that others shared with him in this eschatological event, we need not conclude that Mary, His Mother, was granted a like privilege. But at least it is something to think about. And this is one of the advantages of talking with other Christians about the Christian faith. It makes us think and hopefully think more largely and more charitably."

In the third article, "Fatima and Populorum Progressio," Robert Mollar felt that the relations of Protestants and Catholics in Italy suffered a setback as a result of the Pope's visit to Fatima. Protestants feel that devotion to Mary is extraneous to the gospel and detracts from the faith in Christ. A declaration of Protestant youth stated that Mariology is a barrier to unity because "the unity of the Church may be realized only when all the churches are disposed to recognize that they are in error and forsake the errors of the past in order to turn to their only Lord . . . and allow themselves to be reformed by Him." The Waldensian weekly, *De Luce*, made the observation: "It is clear that according to Paul VI, Mariology is an integral part of the Catholic faith, whether Protestants like it or not. Mary does not belong to the right, but at the center of the Catholic faith . . . and the Mariology of Fatima is not a 'Mariology of the right' which is opposed to the Council's 'Mariology of the left'; both are equally at the center of the Catholic faith . . . and the Mariology of Fatima is not less evangelical—while that of the council is more evangelical—both are equally anti-evangelical."

Dr. Robert McAfee Brown of Stanford University, Palo Alto, California, prominent Presbyterian clergyman and professor, has remarked that Mariology is the area of the greatest theological division between Catholics and Protestants. His opinion is shared by many—

To be sure, the problems of Mariology have not been dissolved by the council. But the discussion has been lifted to a new level. And since Catholics have gone a first mile in trying to reestablish theological *rapport* in this issue, Protestants have an obligation to go a second mile in opening themselves to an examination with their Catholic brethren of what the New Testament says about the place of Mary in Christian faith, and then trying to understand how Catholics can be led beyond that direct evidence to further affirmation that clearly means so much to them in interpreting the signs of God's loving concern for his children.

A further item of ecumenical importance is the inclusion within the constitution of a chapter on Mary. Originally there had been a separate conciliar document on Mary, written in the style of recent papal encyclicals. However, by a very close vote, this council decided to include the Marian material within the context of the materials on the Church, rather than seeming to encourage Marian theology to continue developing in isolation from the rest of Christian thought. The resulting chapter, while still a fully "Catholic" statement, has been rewritten with the ecumenical interest of describing Mary as much as possible in Biblical terms, so that an avenue of possible ecumenical discussion may be opened up. However, not even honest reading will ever provide a full understanding of the faith of the other. This can only come as a *result* of dialogue. For it will only be in some kind of give-and-take, face-to-face encounter, that the most deep-seated misunderstanding will be cleared up. Only as the Protestant is willing to let the Catholic explain, in relation to his own devotional life why Mary is so important to him, will the Protestant really be able to understand existentially the importance of the distinction in Catholic theology between the "worship" of God and the "veneration" of Mary, and avoid the typical Protestant error of confusing the terms. [*Ecumenical Revolution*]

The gap between Protestants and Roman Catholics is wider than that between Roman Catholics and Eastern Orthodox. Many excellent writings by Protestants in recent years attest their loyalty to the Virgin Mary, their appreciation of her role as depicted in the New Testament. They fear, however, that the popular attention devoted to Mary in many areas tends to draw attention from Jesus Christ and that the devotion and veneration now paid to Mary may develop into real worship, and into her exaltation, therefore, both in practice and in theory, to a fully divine role. There are many Catholics who, while not criticizing the doctrines laid down, feel that the emphasis, especially the popular emphasis, on Mariology, the cult of the Virgin, is tending already to distract the minds of believers from the superior and more essential role of her divine Son. It it one thing for Catholics themselves to go as far as their minds and their consciences lead them in their religious practices with regard to the Virgin Mary; it would be quite another thing if they were to insist that all Christians must accept their full doctrine and practice in order to achieve adequate manifestation of Christian unity.

Rev. John Lawson, a Methodist clergyman from England, who once lectured at the Chandler School of Theology at Emory University, Atlanta, set out some of the psychological reasons for Protestant attitudes toward Our Lady, in his article "Mariology: An Irenic Statement." Thus he has stated—

I have already given myself away, I fear, by using for our Lord's Mother the scriptural title "Blessed" (Luke 1:28), by calling her the Virgin, and by putting the word "Mother" with a capital letter! All this will make most Protestants uneasy and give them cause to wonder whether I am in fact a Protestant. It is highly signficant with what cumbrous periphrasis the average Protestant will speak of the mother of Jesus, as though he wished carefully to avoid referring to her with any title of honor. Thus he will say "Mary," but with reluctance "Saint Mary," though he will quite naturally talk about "the Gospel according to St. John." He will say "the mother of Jesus," or if he wishes to be a little more reverential, "the mother of our Lord." But he will not say "the Virgin," still less "the Blessed Virgin," still less "Our Lady," and on no account "the Mother of God." The psychology of this usage is very simple and very natural, though not entirely rational. The Protestant has felt that popular Roman Catholic devotion to the Virgin is excessive, and, despite the disclaimers of Roman theologians, will inevitably be misunderstood among simple people as idolatry. Therefore, he has desired to be as different as possible, in just the same spirit as the Puritans objected to have the Lord's table at the east end of the chancel, because they knew that that was where it stood in a Roman Catholic Church.

However, it is not only simple people who behave like this. Many who pass as responsible Protestant theologians are in a similar emotional prison. One might say that in many academically-minded Protestant circles it has become virtually an act of party-faith passionately to disbelieve in the fact of the virgin birth. This has become a shibboleth. Thus, however much sympathy a

man may profess for modern methods of New Testament exposition in general, if he once declares that he believes in the virgin
birth this alone is enough to brand him as "very conservative,"
and as virtually obscurantist. There is, of course, a clear witness in
the New Testament for the virgin birth, and also undoubted am-
biguities in this evidence. A case can be made either way. It can
hardly be doubted, however, that those who have professed that
love of impartial enquiry which belongs to academic integrity have
found it hard to approach this particular evidence and have come
down with dogmatic force against this particular doctrine because it is to them a convenient mark of difference from Roman
Catholic theology, with its dogmatic attitude. Because Roman
scholars have built this matter up Protestant scholars will make
a particular point of pulling it down, just to show how daring and
independent and un-Roman they are!

He asks Catholics not to take offense but to "remember
that historically Protestants have simply not been able to look
dispassionately on those matters where the theology or devotions of the two faiths divide, any more than the average
modern American can look dispassionately on the respective
merits and demerits of Capitalism and Communism. As your
British forbears and mine faced the Spanish Armada or the
armies of French Louis, Roman Catholicism appeared as the
religion of the enemy. It symbolized a dangerous and cruel
threat to national security. Sympathy with distinctive Roman
Catholics was un-British: and that was that! There was no
necessity to look further. And we are not very far from that
today." Moreover, he suspects that a large part of American
Protestant reserve about Roman Catholicism goes back to
the circumstance that this Church is governed by a hierarchy,
and not by popularly elected representatives. Thus Roman
Catholicism is doubtfully "democratic." This is "un-Ameri-
can" and that is that!

He also observed that among the general body of grass-
roots Protestants and among Protestant theologians to a great
extent,

the real and substantial difficulty about Roman Catholic mariology, is an inherited distaste, emotional and aesthetic rather than

theological or rational, for images, rosaries, candles, genuflections, Ave Marias, and the like.

The Protestant may be assured by the Roman Catholic that all these things are only symbols of unseen spiritual realities, even as the Protestant has his own symbols, and that divine worship is not offered to the Virgin. The Protestant may hear with his ear, and allow his mind to be convinced of the sincerity and rationality of the case, but he cannot constrain his heart to feel. And this latter is the factor which chiefly counts in normal human nature. Thus, although the Protestant may accept the declaration that devotions paid to Our Lady are not idolatry, he will remain convinced that these customs are highly inexpedient in the church because they will be so inevitably and so widely misunderstood as idolatry among simple believers. And I think that the candid Roman Catholic will agree that among simple peasant populations the veneration of saints, angels, and the virgin has often been so misunderstood. To this extent there is force in the objection.

This Methodist theologian notes that it is important for Protestants who take part in ecumenical discussions to realize that they too can easily give offense—

Orthodox Christians who take part in these discussions have often bitterly felt that some of their most sacred devotional sentiments were being affronted by the Protestant's studied avoidance of that language of loving respect which they feel is due to the Virgin. Thus, Protestants, who certainly did not wish to cause any offence and who were sublimely unaware that they were offending, have grieved their Christian brothers. This is the converse of the problem we have discussed above. It has become more pressing since Roman Catholics have taken a more active part in the ecumenical movement. In past years the majority at ecumenical conferences were usually liberal-minded Protestants who worked upon the assumption that liberal-minded Protestantism was the self-evident formula for church unity. The Orthodox were a permanent and long-suffering minority in the meeting. The Roman Catholics we now happily have with us are in a much more commanding position in the West, and Protestants are suddenly beginning to come to a salutary realization that Protestants of all kinds put together are only a minority in the church, and liberal Protestants are only a section of a minority.

In an article, "The Methodist Point of View" (*One in*

Christ, 1967), Rev. Gordon Wakefield of England has pointed out that at first sight there is no devotion to Mary and little teaching about her among Methodists. Lady Day has never been kept, and at Christmas and on Mothering Sunday (fourth Sunday of Lent) Mary is honored as the mother of Jesus but more as a "witness to his true humanity than for her part in redemption."

After showing John Wesley's defense of the virginity of Mary, Dr. Wakefield pointed to Mary's role: "However little we know of her, whatever the precise relations between her and Jesus may have been, however much we may feel unhappy about excessive Marian piety—humanly speaking we owe Jesus principally to his Mother and the more the humanity of Jesus is recognized in its fulness, the more prominent his Mother may become . . ."

He declares that Mary's virginity and motherhood may be a sign of God's independence of ordinary human processes and of proud masculinity. The teaching of the Virgin Birth implies that God achieved His purpose without male desire and did not use the will of man or of the flesh—

> We need to recover the understanding that there is a great deal in life besides sex and that woman is to be honored not simply for the appeal of flesh, but for the distinctly feminine capacities for purity and love.
>
> Mary is ever woman. The New Testament does not record her as divine. She stands with sinners beneath the cross as the representative not of the kingdom of God but of the Church on earth. The words of Christ in the Johannine passion, 'Woman behold thy son,' legitimately allow us to think of Mary as the Mother of the Christian family, the Church—the Church which is left on earth to be the community of the Holy Spirit and a home for all men . . . like all creatures and more than most, she should point us to God. And for too long God has been thought of as a man. If the influence of our mothers, their self-denying love, their bearing with us and yearning over us is so great, how much more must God guard us and care for us and give himself to guide, sustain, protect and save us?

> If Mary be so wonderful,
> What must her Maker be?

The present-day ecumenical climate enabled Cardinal John Carberry of St. Louis thus to address the general conference of the United Methodist Church in Dallas on April 26, 1968—

> One of the blessings of the ecumenical movement is the fact that we can meet and express thoughts which in days gone by we never would have mentioned. I am aware of the traditional Methodist understanding of personal experience, of how God can lead souls to himself in many ways. In the light of this understanding as a help to holiness, I would humbly mention my own personal devotion to Mary, which is a Catholic devotion not widely understood.
>
> Methodists generally recognize that Mary is the most favored of women. In his letter "to a Roman Catholic" John Wesley described her unique status: "I believe that he was made man, joining the human nature with the divine in one person, being conceived by the singular operation of the Holy Ghost and born of the Blessed Virgin Mary, who, as well after as well as before she brought him forth continued a pure and unspotted Virgin."

Dr. Albert Outler of Southern Methodist University was optimistic about the text of chapter 8. "The identification of the Blessed Virgin," he wrote, "as the foremost of all those who have shared in and who still enrich the communion of saints may well have the effect, among other things, of recalling Protestants to an important aspect of Christian faith that they have tended to underestimate in their reaction to what was deemed the excesses of conventional Mariology."

The French Reformed theologian Herbert Roux denied the Virgin Mary any place in the piety of the reformed churches, though he sees her as a splendid type of the human creature, the object of divine grace and redemption, and as an example of humility, hope, and joy in the Lord. He stated that the biblical doctrine of the Blessed Virgin appears to guard against what he calls the fundamental heresy of making this creature, who is the witness of faith in and devotion to the Saviour alone, herself an object of faith and devotion in the Church.

To this I respond that Catholic veneration of Mary is

essentially different from the honor given to God alone. She was not just a kind of biological necessity in the plan of salvation. She shared the life of Jesus; she was associated with His mission. She was present at Cana, on Calvary, and probably on many other occasions. He is called the Son of Mary in Mark's Gospel, and surely the mother of the Messiah is to be accorded special honor and esteem beyond that accorded any other member of the human race.

Roger Schutz, prior of Taize, has asked for

a Protestant effort toward ecumenical understanding of the Virgin Mary. The four centuries have been a part of a conspiracy of silence. We should, however, take into account the weight of a history of more than four centuries, in which, during the course of successive periods, the Virgin Mary has become a subject of opposition and indeed, of segregation among the baptized. In their great care to defend themselves from what they felt to be excessive —in which they at times termed idolatry—in the Catholic attitudes on the Mother of Christ, the Protestants have gone so far as to voice a protest against her.

The Catholics on their part, shocked by what seemed to be going too far, and which they at times deemed sacrilegious in the Protestant reaction, increased their manifestations in honor of the Virgin Mary to the point of creating a state of unbalance within the common realm of piety, hoping by such overdeveloped expressions to make amends for something which wounded their love of the Mother of Christ.

The contemporary religious scene has helped to solve the difficulty. Ecumenism has already created a new attitude on this matter. In the historical Protestant Churches, that old brutal antagonism to the person of the Virgin is no more. Such opposition is restricted to some few circles. Veneration of the Mother of Christ now exists within Protestantism; oftentimes it is related to the affirmation of the role of women in the Church.

As for Catholicism, the contemporary renewal is bringing out an equilibrium between Marian piety and the mystery of Christ and the Church. The last chapter of the *Constitution on the Church* gives testimony of this trend. In considering the relations between Mary and the Church, one begins with an affirmation of Christ the Mediator.

He declares—

our desire to be obedient to Christ in seeking the unity of His

Church requires that we undertake the task of making further steps ahead. Wherefore, we demand from our Catholic and Orthodox brethren that in their devotions, their genuine love of the Mother of Christ be transfigured. We demand that they purify their Marian piety of all extraneous developments so that Virgin Mary will always be kept in that great humility which in the Scriptures distinguishes her in her hidden life at Christ's side.

Humility is Mary's great virtue and should be appreciated by her children—

It is a fact that in Marian piety, anything that would be in the slightest contrary to her role of humility, anything that would be conducive to the expression of that piety in terms of "glorification," would become a barrier and would lead away from that which was the Mother of our Lord.

Mary's depth of prayer comes from her nearness to Christ—

In like manner, it could be that we are too smug in stigmatizing the trust which our Catholic and Orthodox brethren place in the intercession of the Virgin. If we place our trust in those who are dearest to us, asking them to remember us in their prayers, then the refusal to associate in our prayers a person who has gone from our midst would mean putting in doubt the eternal life of those who have attained Christ.

From this standpoint, we can understand the great trust which Catholics have in the continued intercession of the Mother of Christ.

In the early days of the Reformation the conspiracy of silence did not exist. Luther was not aware of a rupture with the whole of the Christian community, and even less of the consequences which we today are experiencing. He venerated the person who was the first to believe in Christ, the first to utter the *yes* and the *amen* of the believing heart, and through whose consent reflected in herself the perfection of Christ.

To realize our will to understand the place of Mary in the Christian community, perhaps we could say together the prayer with which he concludes the article—a prayer to Our Lady used by the monks of Taize—

Holy and merciful Father, you have revealed to the Blessed Virgin Mary that through the coming of her Son, the powerful would be brought low and the humble exalted. We pray for the humbled who with her cry to you.

O Christ, you who were born of the Virgin Mary, who was obedient to your word, grant to us also the spirit of prompt obedience. With her, the first of the whole cloud of witnesses, we want to learn to say to you: be it done to me according to your will.

O God, you willed to make of the Virgin Mary the figure of the Church. She has received Christ, and she has given him to the world. Send down upon us the Holy Spirit, so that we might soon be visibly united in one sole body, and that we might radiate Christ upon the men who are unable to believe.

Gather us all together in visible unity so that with the Virgin Mary and all the holy witnesses of Christ we may rejoice in you, our Saviour, now, always and in eternity, (*Unité Chrétienne,* May, 1967, p. 3)

Canon Bernard Pawley, an Anglican observer at the Council, is equally laudatory, addressing a British Anglican gathering: ". . . what we should recognize as very adequate and commendable treatment to the knotty problem of the place of the Blessed Virgin Mary in the Christian economy. . . . I hope you will read the Constitution on the Church and all the other decrees as they come out, so that you can explain them to your Roman Catholic neighbor, in case he hasn't read them. I hope you will find that considering the point from which they started and the opposition against which they had to fight the liberals of the Council have done a very good job indeed, if I may say so, on the figure of the Blessed Virgin Mary."

Victor de Wall gave an Anglican reaction with an eye to the Eastern churches. He finds chapter 8 balanced and admirable, "combining as it does an insistence on the sole mediatorship of Jesus Christ with the affirmation that Our Lady is the sign that within the Church all the people of God are called to participate in the work of their redemption." Many Anglicans, "even of Protestant inclinations," have found the Marian devotion of the Eastern churches more attractive than that of Western Catholicism because of the liturgical context of the piety of the East, "where there is less sense of dogmatic speculation than of participation with the whole

Church triumphant in the praise of the Blessed Trinity." It was in this direction, he continued, that this chapter of the Constitution seemed to be pointing. What brief attention the World Council of Churches has so far given to "Mary in the communion of saints" has come from Orthodox insistence, beginning with S. Bulgalov's intervention at the first Faith and Order Conference in Lausanne in 1927, insisting that the role of Mary in the plan of salvation should be discussed. This development is discussed in *The Ways of Worship* (London, 1947), in which there are three articles dealing with Mary in the Catholic, the Orthodox, and the Protestant, or Reformed, tradition.

The American Episcopalian layman William Stringfellow has judged that the Vatican Council was badly wanting in respect to Mariology. Before chapter 8 was published, he is reported to have said ". . . there is only one serious theological obstacle to organic reunion, and that is the doctrine and cult of Mary. That seems to be the last important barrier between some of the rest of us and the Roman Church." After the document was published, Stringfellow expressed his view in the article "A Protestant's Disenchantment," as part of *A Pessimist's Guide to the Vatican Council.* His sentiments were pesimistic indeed: "Evidently that most delicate issue, regarding Mary, the Mother of Jesus, is to be also neglected by the Council, though, without clarification of the doctrine of Mary, there is no hope at all for the reunion of the Church."

Perhaps his writing reflected his mood at the time. He seemed to be against Mary as well as against the Catholic doctrine and veneration of her. He asked for "a better reliance upon the authority of the Bible in understanding Mary," but then made the gratuitous assumption: "If recourse is had to the New Testament, Mary emerges as one who was both extraordinarily possessive toward her Son and consistently opposed to his vocation."

This opinion differed vastly from the statements of chapter 8: "She is hailed as the pre-eminent exemplar in faith and charity. Taught by the Holy Spirit, the Catholic Church shows filial devotion to her as a most loving Mother" (art. 53). Or in another place: "With no sin to hamper her, she whole-heartedly embraced God's salvific will, devoted herself completely as the Lord's handmaid to the person and work of her Son, and through the grace of Almighty God served the mystery of redemption under him and with him" (art. 56). Little wonder that Stringfellow finds Mary such an obstacle. But I think there is a preconception that gives rise to such a position, and to that we must listen too.

According to Bishop John E. Hines, presiding bishop of the Episcopal Church in the United States, the problems inherent in papal infallability are demonstrated by the dogmas on Mary, for example the Assumption (defined Nov. 1, 1950, by Pope Pius XII). "We are willing to pay her honor," he asserted, "but many of us think the Roman Catholic Church has moved beyond the biblical interpretation."

In a book by Lutherans on the Vatican Council, *The Way of Dialogue,* Dr. Warren Quanbeck of the Lutheran Theology Seminary, St. Paul, Minnesota, devoted a chapter to Mary. He expressed apprehension about the role of Mary in Catholic devotion and practice. The place of Mary is "one of the most sensitive topics." He stated that the Catholic suspects that the Protestant lacks realism, while the Protestant fears that the Catholic has confused Christology, ecclesiology, and Mariology.

He maintained that the Church must confess that Mary is Theotokos, Mother of God. The definition of 431, he concluded, was primarily a statement not about Mary but about her Son. "Jesus Christ is the only Mediator, he is the word of God, the Reconciler, the Redeemer. He brings God to us and He is sufficient. Emphasis upon Mary the Mother of God is not a move to displace Him but to ensure His solidarity with us as the Word became flesh. Mary stands in the Christian tradition as the assurance of the humanity of Jesus, the reality of his life on earth: Jesus the Christ toiled, sweat, knew weariness, disappointment and defeat. Four centuries of history of

Protestantism should make us wary of rejecting too quickly the importance of Mary in the work of salvation."

In his comment on chapter 8, Dr. Quanbeck found the document impressive for its use of Scripture "and in its attempt to bring to focus the biblical teaching on Mary and to do so in terms of sound exegesis." For him it stressed the mediation of Christ and Mary's function in relation to Christ and the Church.

On the negative side he found the document not the best of the council, "not even very good." There is no definition of the role of Mary in Redemption, he states, and "the Protestant reader is left with the disquieting sense that neither the dogmatic nor liturgical *caveats* are sufficient." He also finds that the theological language is not as biblical and patristic as it might be. "It dramatizes the painful consequences of centuries of separation and how much discussion is needed before various church groups even understand each other, much less make common progress in theological studies. It is a later and not altogether satisfactory beginning of an effort to do this, but in our ecumenical poverty even a beginning is an occasion for thanks to God."

Oscar Cullman, the Swiss theologian, contributed an article, "The Bible in the Council." He dissented strongly from what he calls the non-contextual use of Scripture in the chapter. "Here texts are cited," he averred, "whose basic meaning has nothing to do with the statements of the schema and which have been inserted into the document only as afterthoughts." And concerning the claim that the Assumption is "implicitly" in the Bible, Cullman remarks, ". . . if the bodily assumption of Mary really is implicitly in the Bible, then I really don't know what is not implicitly in the Bible. I must admit that in this case I prefer the theory of the conservative Catholics who flatly affirm that the Assumption is not in the Bible, but only in tradition, except that I would add that this is a deviant tradition." The question here devolves on the meaning of tradition and its role in revelation. Protestants generally do not assign the same role to the Church Fathers that Catholics and Orthodox do; this is one reason for the difficulty, though it is not an insuperable one.

But if also in other uses the Council makes of the bible for Our Lady (as Mark 3 and Luke 11), then, even more basically, what authority has the Council concerning the revealed word? Perhaps most crucial of all, what is Mary's *present* place in the communion of the saints? On earth, as the Scriptures show, she was the model of faith, hope, and charity; but what does she mean *now?* The whole concept of Mary is under scrutiny—not just her role in the Scriptures but her role in the whole life of the Church as well.

"Communion of saints" is a credal Christian inheritance; all churches have a long way to go until they will be one in understanding and accepting of this truth. The publication *Living Room Dialogues: A Guide for Lay Discussion. Catholic-Orthodox-Protestant,* edited by W. B. Greenspun, C.S.P., and W. A. Norgren, and published jointly by the Paulist Press and the National Council of Churches, puts two crucial questions under the heading "Our Common Christian Heritage." The questions are relevant, and the answers will be revealing: *"For Catholics:* do you sometimes in your devotions replace Jesus with the Virgin Mary or with the saints? Give reason for your answer. *For Protestants:* do you think your personal relationship with Christ would be incomplete if Mary, the saints and the other members of the Church were completely excluded from it? Give reasons for your answers."

The late Dr. Douglas Horton, an American observer at the Council, thought that one emphasis made again and again mystified most observers—

Mary was spoken of as the harbinger of church union. One bishop held that Marian doctrine had given rise to the ecumenical movement. He asserted (with what justification I cannot guess) that after each papal definition of the status of Mary, this movement had gained strength. It is known that the Eastern Churches venerate Mary but they do not seem to regard her as the palladium of ecumenicity. The one speaker who pointed out that the "founder of Protestantism" (meaning, I gather, Martin Luther) held her in veneration, was surely under a delusion if he thought that Protestant Christianity had accepted and developed this type of devotion. Protestant thinkers are beginning to take up the subject of Mariology with far more seriousness than they ever have in the past, but to regard Mary as an ecumenical figure for today is surely to misapprehend the temper of contemporary non-Roman Christianity.

One Lutheran said to Dr. Horton:

These are the darkest days of the council. I never felt so far from Rome as I do now. Strangely enough the Eastern Orthodox do not seem to be any happier, for though they make Mary the object of devotion, they seem definitely adverse to theologizing about her. It would be profitable for the larger Christian dialogue if the council would make the most precise statement it can regarding the values and limits of Marian devotion, but it is equally important for Rome to know that other Christians feel a sufficiency in Christ, witnessed to by the Holy Spirit.

Elsewhere Dr. Horton made this observation of Marian devotion—

No end of praises were thrown, like garlands, at Mary's feet. She is before the church, because she was created before the church. She portrays all the virtues. She is the temple of the Holy Spirit in a peculiar way and it is no wonder that the separated brethren sometimes think that we attribute to Mary many characteristics of the Holy Spirit since they are so closely associated. She is the "second Eve," the spiritual mother of all the living. It seemed that for a great many of the council fathers no superlative of excellence was too brilliant to add to Mary's crown.

One of my colleagues later observed that this kind of adulation really has no limits for once you are airborne above the facts of history, there is no obstacle to arrest your flight into space. This is true beyond doubt, but the fact that so many mature men have allowed themselves to become thus airborne is a matter of significance in itself. It will hardly do for those of us who stick to the facts of history to wave our heads at this imaginative type of worship; as students of human nature we shall simply have to ask why Mary has come to exert such a powerful and portentous influence over so many people.

Why some theologians and authors get "airborne" in regard to Our Lady, I am not certain. Some exuberance is a

kind of poetry. And while not excusing the excess, I note that
this tendency has existed in the Christian Church for centuries.
I do not defend it; I am trying to explain why it exists. Even
today the writings of Italy, Spain, and Latin countries are,
generally speaking, different from those of the United States
and England. There are poetical figures of speech, there is a
rhetoric not meant to be strictly theological, to be found in
prayers such as the *Salve Regina* of the eleventh century and
the *Memorare* (not from St. Bernard of Clairvaux but from a
French priest). This recalls the remark of St. Bernard of
Toledo: "For your sake, O Mary, the scriptures were written;
because of you the world was made." Again, I do not defend
but explain. The remark can be interpreted as meaning the eternal predestination of Mary together with the Incarnate Word
and in a secondary sense could apply to Mary. But I concede
that it seems ambiguous and should not be used, unless qualified, and that in the interest of ecumenism such statements
should be replaced.

Teilhard de Chardin was deeply devoted to the Virgin
Mary. He was attracted to the teaching of the Immaculate
Conception, no doubt because of the peerless purity of Our
Lady, an idea that he refers to and develops in various places.
The Immaculate Conception was his favorite feast of Our
Lady. He loved the rosary and prayed it daily. He was fond
of saying that it was necessary for man to become refined,
sensitive, and human in order to love Our Lady deeply.

Mary was for Teilhard the epitome of purity, beauty, and
simplicity. She was the creation of God's interest in the world
through whom the Word would become incarnate. All of human life is christianized in many by a development of the
Hail Mary. For Teilhard this prayer was a kind of synthesis of
Our Lady's life and devotion; man would be a Christian to the
extent that he lived this prayer in his own existence. Man
needs to be "interested" in his fellow man and in God, as
Mary was; he needs to "sympathize" with her, to know her
better; and as the heart of the Virgin becomes transparent to
those who love her, so man must see that all the Christian

mysteries are familiar, concrete, and real in the Virgin. Teilhard liked to speak of the faith of Mary too, as the result of her purity. His students and his thought must take into account his recognition of Our Lady in order to understand his stress on the mystery of the Incarnation. They must also see him as a man of deep faith, whose model of prayer and virtue is Our Lady, the humble maid of Nazareth and the mother of the Lord.

While developing this thought of Mary's role in human history, we might pay brief tribute to the apostles and prophets of Christian unity who were conscious of Mary's part in ecumenism. Abbe Paul Couturier, (1870–1953) of Lyons, France, promoted the Week of Prayer for Christian Unity throughout much of Europe, while Father Paul James Francis, S.A. (1863-1940), began the Unity Octave in 1908 in the United States and did much to promote it in his own country and throughout the English-speaking world. The French priest saw Mary as *the* example of prayer for unity—

Let all Christians approach their Lord Christ, with hearts open and attentive to the divine call in an attitude of humble abandonment following the example of Mary's humility. She replied to the angel in the archetypal words of the creature to the Creator: "Behold the handmaid of the Lord. Be it done to me according to His word." When the attitude of Christians is that of Mary, when the Virgin's reply echoes silent in the hearts of us all, this vast silent prayer, guided and led by the voice of the Virgin, will break like a wave before the throne of God in an irresistible supplication. And once again there will be unity, "by the action of the Holy Spirit."

How could she who on earth said to her Son: "They have no more wine," not say to Him in heaven: "They no longer have unity"? And seeing that she stood at the foot of His cross, her heart at one with that of the Lamb's in his supplication to His Father for the unity of the whole Christian family: "Father, let them be one as we are one."

Let all Christians join her and listen to her as she stands at the foot of the cross and at the feet of the Lamb.

In 1949 Father Couturier made on offering of his whole life for unity, through the love of Our Lady. "O holy Virgin

Mary, if, in spite of promises or donations made in days gone by, you still leave me free to offer, in your maternal hands, my agony and death as a supreme supplication for Christian Unity, I do so with great gratitude. I hope that you will be well disposed to my wish and that, through you, this last earthly supplication will be accepted by Jesus, your Son, the Christ my Saviour." He left this prayer on the altar where he had offered Mass for the last time.

Father Paul of Graymoor was also deeply devoted to Our Lady for the cause of Christian unity. From the first days of his foundation at Graymoor he promoted a strong and confident love for the Mother of God. He began the title of and devotion to Our Lady of the Atonement in 1900 or 1901. When he first conceived the idea of the Unity Octave in November, 1908, he was the founder of the Society of the Atonement. He was an Anglican until he and his small community were received into the Catholic Church at Graymoor on October 30, 1909. The Missionary Congress met in Edinburgh in 1910 under the leadership of John Mott, Bishop Charles Brent, and Bishop Nathan Soderblom, and this is usually considered the beginning of the present-day ecumenical movement.

Father Paul originated the Feast of Our Lady of the Atonement to promote love for Mary as a means of fostering religious unity. His first writing on this theme was in *Rose Leaves,* a monthly publication at Graymoor, in its maiden issue of October, 1901. He stated clearly—

The Blessed Virgin is known among Catholics by many names and invoked under many titles. Famous among these are the following: Our Lady of Grace, Our Lady of Sorrows, Our Lady of Mercy. In her wonderful condescension and love the Mother of God has been pleased to reveal herself to the Children of the Atonement under a new name, thus giving remarkable evidence that the honor, love and prayers to her as OUR LADY OF THE ATONEMENT she is graciously pleased to accept. We have every reason to believe that the Blessed Virgin specially loves this title that links her name with that of Jesus in the glorious work of the Atonement wrought upon the Cross. It must bring to her remembrance of that blessed Atonement Day when she stood by the Cross of Jesus and heard Him say to her: "Woman, behold thy son," and to the disciple whom He loved: "Behold, thy Mother." Then too Atonement speaks of reconciliation, pardon, peace, of the fulfillment of the prayer, first breathed by her Divine Son, so often repeated by herself, that Christian believers might be One.

Can we invoke the Blessed Virgin with a title more apt to touch her maternal heart than the one which associates her with Calvary's sacrifice and proclaims her the compassionate Mother of us poor sinners, redeemed by the Precious Blood of Jesus? Hail Mary of the Atonement, my Lord's Mother and mine, pray for me and all who thus invoke thee now and at the hour of our death. Amen.

Later, Father Paul expressed this concept of his duty to promote love for Our Lady of the Atonement as a special means of effecting the desired Christian unity—

Our mission is not only to preach Christ crucified, but also to promote and extend devotion to Our Lady of the Atonement . . . until a vast number of the faithful shall be united with Our Lady of the Atonement, our Mother in heaven, in the work of prayer and intercession for the conversion of the whole world to Christ, so that the Passion and Atoning Sacrifice of our Divine Redeemer may be made effectual to the fullest extent in the salvation of souls and in the completion of the number of God's elect.

In many letters and articles towards the last years of his life, Father Paul said that he hoped that devotion to Our Lady of the Atonement would become universal. In a letter to Bishop Georges Caruana, apostolic nuncio in Cuba, he related: "We pray that like Church Unity the devotion to our Blessed Lady as our Atonement Mother will spread more universally from the Graymoor hearth to the four corners of the earth, and that by its influence the Atoning Sacrifice of the New Law will the more speedily dominate the children of the earth in accordance with our Lord's prayer: 'That all may be one.' "

An Anglican book, *The Blessed Virgin Mary*, has a chapter on "Our Lady and the Reunion of Christendom," by Augustine Morris, O.S.B., abbot of Nashdom. He wrote: "If still in heaven Jesus our Lord in his sacred humanity 'ever liveth to make intercession for us,' then she who of all the human race is far closest to him shares in that continuing intercession. If still in heaven he prays his high-priestly prayer, 'that all may be one,' then she, whose will is wholly united with his, offers the same prayer for all those whom he has committed to her charge."

Karl Barth has said, "The Mother of God of Roman Catholic dogma is quite simply the principle, the prototype and the epitome of the human creature cooperating in salvation with the aid of grace which assists it; as such she is the principle, prototype and epitome of the Church." I would agree with two of his terms, "prototype" and "epitome," but not with the concept of principle, unless of course he had a different meaning for this word than is usually given to it.

Bishop Theas of Lourdes pointed to this role of Mary when he welcomed Anglican pilgrims to "The City of Mary" in August, 1963—

> All men, especially all those who are baptized, are called to live in a family, the family of the children of God. A family that is truly united fulfills the plan of God, and assures the happiness of its members. The great sorrow of Christians, and this is felt and regretted by all, is the dissensions that exist among them. But in a family, is it not the role of a mother to bring together her scattered children and, as she looks on them with her gracious smile, to reconcile them and to make them love each other? The greatest happiness of a mother is in the unity of her children. Was not the Virgin Mary given the mission of uniting us to Jesus, of uniting us all in Jesus? Is it not her office to be, as St. Augustine said, "Mother of Unity"?
>
> If they would achieve the unity which Jesus desires, Christians should first of all go together to Mary's maternal heart, so that, in their Mother's company, they may discover together the wonders of her Son's plan, as He calls men to lead a fraternal life and, by keeping close to Mary, the universal Mother, they find opportunities of coming together, of understanding each other, of showing mutual kindness and friendship.

Bishop Theas took the gilded statue of Mary and placed it in the hands of the Anglican Bishop of Chidilton. Catholics and Anglicans sang the Magnificat together, and then, at the Anglican bishop's request, Bishop Theas blessed the pilgrims.

Harvey Cox, Baptist, who enjoys wide popularity in the United States, has referred to Mary in the context of the feminine image now current in advertising circles. "Just as the Virgin appears in many guises," he wrote, "as Our Lady of Lourdes or of Fatima or of Guadalupe, but is always recognizably the Virgin, so with the Girl [as idealized for modern man]. During the classical Christian centuries the Virgin Mary served in part as this model. With the Reformation and especially with the Puritans, the place of Mary within the symbol of the Protestant countries was reduced or eliminated." He poses the question: "Why had Protestantism kept its attention obsessively fastened on the development of Mariolatry in Catholicism and not noticed the sinister rise of the vampire cult of the Girl in our society? . . . The Girl is a far more pervasive destructive influence and it is to her and her omnipresent altar that we should be directing our criticism."

What his psychological explanations may be there is no sure way of knowing. The comparison is at best naive and very crude. The image of Mary in Christian thought and devotion is hardly to be compared with the image of the Girl (or Woman) used in today's world of mass-media communication, in nearly every form of promotion and advertising, in sports, et cetera. This composite is hardly to be given the same consideration or evaluation in culture—or in the lack of it—as the Mother of God by any comparison. Religion is surely not to be confused with materialistic or non-Christian psychology and sociology.

The following insight seems to favor genuine devotion to Mary and hence the reunion of Christians. She is the figure of the Church's mission in the world. Obviously the mission of the Church is not just to build up from without, to increase its membership. Nor is it to coerce people morally or physically. Rather it is to bear witness to faith, hope, and love. The Church is the sacrament of Christ's presence in the world. Mary is a special model and pattern of this mission. She conceived Him both in body and in mind, she carried Him in joyous "haste into the hill country" (a symbol of the resistance and obstacles of this world). She was present when Jesus offered himself on the cross and present too where the Spirit was working (Luke 1:35; Acts 1:14) and finally present among men as the perfect figure of the Church's mission and the mission of every Christian. A Protestant clergyman asked when I spoke of Mary and the Church: "Does that mean Mary and Catholic charities?" Not necessarily, I thought, but there is no greater model for this operation than Our Lady; and if this were the motivation, how spiritually alive such a program could be!

In Darmstadt, Germany, there is a Lutheran sisterhood established in honor of Our Lady. Their idea is to pray and work for unity and to carry on an apostolate under the inspiration of the Blessed Virgin. One phase of their work is to maintain a rest home for elderly Jews in Jerusalem, to atone for the Nazi outrages against the Jews. The costs are covered by contributions mostly from Denmark, Switzerland, and Germany. It is a practical work of service done in the name of Mary.

The Moslems have a high regard for Mary, or Miriam as they call her. There are several references to her in the Koran; and while the Moslem concept of Our Lady is different from the Catholic devotion to her, still this common love can help to bring about a better relationship between the members of the two faiths. The references in the Koran are to the mother of Jesus, the Annunciation, the Visitation and the birth of Jesus. (Some have thought that mention is made of the Immaculate Conception, but this seems unlikely, at least in the theological sense of the Catholic Church.)

Jesus is repeatedly called "the son of Mary." The following excerpt is from Surah III: "And when the angels said: O Mary! Lo! Allah hath chosen thee and made thee pure and hath preferred thee above [all] the women of creation.

"O Mary! Be obedient to thy Lord, prostrate thyself and bow with those who bow [in worship], . . . [And remember] when the angels said: O Mary! Lo! Allah giveth thee glad tidings of a word from Him, whose name is the Messiah Jesus, son of Mary, illustrious in the world and in the hereafter, and one of those brought near [unto Allah]."

Moslem women are known to ask Catholic and Orthodox priests to pray to Mary for them, especially in childbirth. The Moslem love of Mary may not be the tender sentiment of the Christian tradition, particularly among the men, but there is a sense of veneration and esteem which must be considered in the relationship of Christians and Moslems. "And Mary, daughter of 'Imram, whose body was chaste, therefore We breathed therein something of our Spirit. And she put faith in the words of her Lord and His Scriptures and was of the obedient." (66:12.)

Prior to his visit to Fatima in 1967, the Holy Father stated that he hoped a common love for Our Lady would help promote unity among the churches of East and West. He desired that the exhortation to love Mary would be received by "those who, while not enjoying full communion with the Catholic Church, nevertheless, together with us admire and venerate the handmaid of the Lord, the Virgin Mary, Mother of the Son of God."

In this context I should like to refer to the thought of Dr. Jaroslav Pelikan, mentioned earlier. In the preface to Otto Semmelroth, S.J., *Mary, Archetype of the Church,* Professor Pelikan observed: "The current vogue of the phrase 'separated brethren' may blunt the sense of loss it is intended to voice: recognition that the walls of separation do not reach to heaven may reduce the urgency of doing something about the walls of earth. . . . There still remains the scandal that brethren who have God as their Father and Christ as their Elder Brother should be separated as they are in their attitude toward Mary as the Mother of God."

Christian unity must be involved in devotion to and esteem for Our Lady. If love for Mary means the imitation of her virtues and a growth in holiness, then surely it will foster the unity of all men in Christ. On this point Renè Laurentin has

declared: "Devotion to the Blessed Virgin must be inspired
by the goal of unity and efficacy in pursuit of salvation . . .
[she has] that universal and unifying place which is hers in the
Church, a place where her presence will stimulate demands and
Christian initiative, a presence whose sole purpose is to lead
us to the fulness of Christ."

It is a mistake to suppose that Catholics can promote the
ecumenical movement by putting Our Lady aside as if she
were an embarrassment or an obstacle to be ignored. Ul-
timately unity will be achieved by a convergence of all Christians upon the wholeness of truth in love, and there is nothing
to be gained by minimizing or exaggerating any one truth, and
especially that of Mary.

Christian unity is the work of the Blessed Trinity—of the
Father, the Son, and the Holy Spirit. It is an achievement so
supernaturally wonderful and compelling that it will convince
the world of the message and mission of the Saviour. Though
Christians are to cooperate to bring about the desired goal, it
will be God's achievement, not man's, and it will come according to His will and His grace.

What we must pray for and seek for is the extension of
divine truth and holiness in human life so as to transform the
world. One truth is that God honored the Virgin Mary above
all creatures even as He asked more from her in sorrow and
sacrifice. We can never honor her as much as God has, but we
must esteem the role that He has given to her.

Mary is the Mother of unity because she is the Mother of
Christ and He is the central principle of unity. I agree that
Christian unity will come as men succeed in bringing themselves to Christ, forgetful of self, of pride and ambition, seeking only to do His will by knowing too that we can find it
only as He gives man the grace to do so. They are completely
dependent on Jesus for guidance and strength in the search
for unity.

Mary is our model in the holy enterprise of unity. Her
whole being was concentrated at all times on the perfect doing of God's will and of God-in-Christ. We cannot fully com-

prehend the utter self-donation, the fullness of trust, contained in her words: "Be it done unto me according to Thy Word." Mary accepted completely all the fearful sacrifice of self that was to be the lifelong commitment of her from whom the Word took His human nature.

Mary is the Mother of unity because Jesus made Himself her Son. Since this is so, we can move onward to Christian unity through her inspiration and prayerful love. Mary is the one means by which the union of God with man was brought about through the Incarnation. She lived and suffered in union with Him, the Redeemer of the world.

Mary, then, is the complete opposite of an obstacle or stumbling block to Christian unity. The difficulty is caused by misrepresentation of her and of her role in the divine plan. Such misrepresentation must be corrected. But Mary must receive from us what God wills that she receive in love and honor. We must conform ourselves to the divine will, which is the only way to Christian unity.

Christians must imitate Mary in her oneness with God, in her love for Him, in her prayers for others. In this way, they will do much to attain Christian unity.

I wish to refer now to a paper by the late Cardinal Bea, whose name in ecumenism is held in the highest regard. In a recent book, *The Way to Unity After the Council,* he devoted a chapter to "Marian Doctrine and Devotion in Harmony with the Ecumenical Spirit." He wrote that "among the greatest blessings bestowed on the Church in recent years are the Mariological and ecumenical movements." He quoted with approval the words of Pope Leo XIII: "The greatest safeguard for Christian unity is to be found in Mary." He urged both sides not to give in to extremes, either in eulogizing Mary beyond what Scripture and normative teaching have proposed or in minimizing Mary's role. When we consider her not only as honored by Christ but also as His handmaid, as she spoke of herself, we see her in the service of the Redemption. "She is brought much nearer to us and not left on a distant pedestal with such a wealth of special graces as to seem self-sufficient. Like the Redeemer himself she can be seen serving and helping all mankind. It also forestalls many of the preconceived objections that might come from Christians of other persuasions against a special type of veneration arising from her unique role in the work of redemption, as *Alma socia Redemptoris*."

The venerable Cardinal added—

> . . . authentic circumspect and profound devotion to the Blessed Mother, harmoniously united to a deep longing for Christian unity, is something that cannot be achieved overnight. It presupposes a profound understanding of Catholic doctrine as handed down and expounded slowly but surely over the centuries; it presupposes, further, a broad view of the rich and rightful range of Marian devotions at different times and places with due allowance for exaggerations, deviations, corruptions, misunderstandings, and even frauds which the weakness of human nature has unfortunately rendered unavoidable in this as in other branches of the Church's life.
>
> Only an extended and accurate familiarity with sound doctrine and Marian devotion through the ages can help us to find the correct solution for the thorny problems presented to all who endeavor to unite in complete harmony an authentic love and veneration for Mary with an ardent and active apostolate for the union of all believers in Christ.

It seems to me that we are witnessing in the Church and in the churches today a deeper and more extensive reverence for the Virgin Mary. It is part of Catholic teaching but it is also the heritage of the other Christian churches, as pointed out by the leaders I have referred to, as well as by Max Thurian, Pastor Jean Bosc, and others. "The theology of the reformers shows an interest in Mary, and in her role and meaning; this interest is clearly positive and is to be contrasted with the reticence or even complete silence which later Protestantism was to have over the Virgin as an anti-Catholic reaction . . . it remains to be said, however, that the positive aspects of this Mariology should and could be given a more fully real place in the life of the Church," the Cardinal wrote.

In another context the Cardinal affirmed Mary's role in reunion—

What aspect does the human family present to the eyes of Our Lady today? That of lamentable divisions. Almost nine hundred millions of Christians are scattered over the face of the earth—and yet how unhappily they are divided. . . . How far away in the eyes of Our Lady is the Christian family from that perfect unity which Jesus asked His Father a few hours before He gave up his life for us when He prayed: "That all may be one. . . ." Jesus also said: "A new commandment I give you, that you love one another as I have loved you." Alas, between one group of Christians and another how many prejudices, suspicions, resentments, aversions! Think for a moment of the sorrow this causes the heavenly Mother, who is the Mother of all Christians! How deeply she must feel this separation between sons of the heavenly Father and brothers of her only Son." [Sermon at Fatima, May, 1963.]

On the same occasion he spoke of the meaning of devotion to Our Lady, to lead to union with Christ—

Here you have the true significance of our devotion to Our Lady— intimate union with Christ and consequently the loftiest heights of achievement in our apostolate to which this union can and will bring us. Our devotion thus understood and practiced will truly please Christ and God for humanity.

And so this splendid pilgrimage of today, besides its immediate fruit—this great and most precious capitol of prayer and penance for the important intentions of the Church—will bring other results even still more lasting. In the school of Mary and in union with Mary we will see our life transformed into a living image of Christ Himself for our good and for the good of the Church, for the salvation of so many souls and for the greater glory of God.

All of human life is a pilgrimage, to the final destination of heaven. Human life, the existence of the Church, human striving and effort, are ordained to the ultimate end that God has established for man. It is not the role of Mary to impede the process or the progress but to promote it and to facilitate it. She does so in a motherly way, with patience, love, and prayer for her children, who are the members of her Son.

The thought of Renè Laurentin is filled with promise and with hope. Genuine love of Mary does not create annoyance and tension. It may mean adjustment, but this will help maintain the balance. "It gives us a glimpse of the end of the road, whose meanderings we cannot trace: the communion of all in one renewed doctrine and piety, where the Virgin, no longer pulled in conflicting directions, will be restored to that universal and unifying place which is hers in the Church, a place where her presence will stimulate Christian demands and Christian initiative, a presence whose whole purpose is to lead us to the fullness of Christ."

6

THE FUTURE OF MARIOLOGY

In this period of change in the Church as well as in all society it might seem rather over ambitious or foolish to attempt any assessment of Marian thought and devotion. But I think that chapter 8 of the Constitution points the way. The role of Mary will grow more prominent, and not through a proliferation of titles or of devotional practices but through a deeper understanding of her position and function in the mystery of Christ and in the mystery of the Church. She will be seen in the light of the Church itself, as the type of the Church, the model of every Christian, bringing the brethren of her Son closer to one another and to God by her love and intercession and by her example. She herself followed the pilgrimage of faith that led to everlasting glory.

Mary is in the Mystical Body of her Son. She is the first member of holiness just as Peter is the first member in the ministry of the Church on earth. She is part of the Church, not isolated from it; and as Pope Paul VI says, she is "the greatest part, the best part, the principal part, the chosen part."

Mary's privileges, which are in close dependence on Christ himself, are a high compliment to human nature, for the mother of the Lord was a member of the human race. God's selection of her for His purpose is also a manifestation of His preference for the poor and the lowly, the *anawim*. She is the handmaid of the Lord, the slave girl of God.

This person, "blessed among women," was a poor, simple woman involved in all the want, hard work, oppression, and uncertainty about the future that are inseparable from life in any undeveloped area. In Nazareth a woman's work was a struggle for existence from dawn until night. Mary had not only to wash and mend clothes but to weave the cloth and spin the yarn. She ground the flour to bake the bread; she may have had to cut the firewood. That, at least, is what the women of Nazareth are doing in our own day.

Mary was no queen of an earthly kingdom. She was the wife and mother of workingmen. She was poor and lowly, for this was the state chosen by the Son of God, and it was her calling to give birth to Him and thus provide the introduction of His place in the history of mankind. It was necessary that she share with Him the state of drudgery and oppression common to the vast majority He came to redeem, those "who labor and are heavily burdened" (Matt. 11:28). "It was necessary that Christ should suffer" (Luke 24:26) and die. And so it was necessary that the Mother of God should be the mother of a man condemned to death with all the shame brought on Him by the hostility of the people and the religious and civil authorities of the country in which He lived.

This low estate with which Jesus involved Himself is the root of His mother's glory. It is the law of the Magnificat (Luke 1:48) and of the beatitudes (Matt. 5:3-11; Luke 6: 20-22). We should not conceive of Mary as a kind of spiritual fairy godmother, or far-off princess in a never-never land. Mary is highest in grace, but she is one of human nature. She must have known better than anyone the meaning of the Saviour's words: "When you have done all that is commanded you, say: 'We are unworthy servants, we have only done what was our duty' " (Luke 17:10). The only title she gave herself was "handmaid," and she uses it twice (Luke 1:38,48). She is the mother of Him who assumes the servants' apron to serve those who are ready to serve Him (Luke 12:37, 22:27; John 13:1-16).

The Mariology of the future will be more biblical, patristic, ecclesiological, and ecumenical. It will be more Christocentric and liturgical. Devotion to Mary will be not simply a prayer of praise or petition but an imitation of her faith, her humility, her poverty, her service in love toward the members of Christ.

Pope Paul VI sounded this note in the Mariological Congress of Santo Domingo of February 2, 1965: "Strive for a deepening of the knowledge and love of the mysteries of Mary rather than for an effort at theological extension, sometimes subject to discussion and calcuated to divide souls rather than to unite them . . . to moderate an unbalanced and unenlightened sentimentalism . . . and encourage a series and living devotion which is at home in the great unitive plan of the liturgy."

Renè Laurentin has suggested a threefold program in developing proper Marian thought and devotion: (1) resumption of contact with the East; (2) recognition of the Holy Spirit in the Church; and (3) a deeper understanding of Mary's presence.

I think that Catholic contact should be intensified not only with the East, with both Eastern Catholics and the Orthodox, but also with those Protestants who by their study and work contribute much to the integration of Christian thought and life.

The Holy Spirit must be accorded His place in the Church and in the plan of salvation. If the Spirit is forgotten or neglected, the Mystical Body has no meaning, for the principle of unity is ignored. Christ would be the head of the Body, but the Body would be impersonal and inorganic.

The Holy Spirit is the bond of unity between the Father and the Son; He is the principle of unity in the Church. Mary is bound to the Holy Spirit in a unique way—in the Annunciation, on Calvary, and at Pentecost. Mary is the privileged witness and sign of the Holy Spirit. She was with the infant Church on Pentecost, which received the Spirit in a special way; she has the primary place in the communion of saints in heaven.

Mary is the ally of the Holy Spirit and acts as a catalyst for the action by which the Holy Spirit identifies the members of the Church with Christ and inspires in them enthusiasm, joy, and His fruits, even as He led the Virgin Mary over the hill country of Galilee when she visited Elizabeth and sang her incomparable hymn, the Magnificat. Mary is entirely related to the Holy Spirit, for she is entirely related to Christ.

The third point is Mary's presence in the Church: The basis of this presence is her presence in the life of Christ. Mary was with Him more than anyone else during His entire incarnate life, from the first moment of existence until His death on the cross. This presence included times of joy and sorrow, of trial and of loss. She was separated from Him in the Temple, during the time (or some of it) of His public life, and the period between Calvary and the Assumption. The material loss only deepened the communion of grace during the time of absence. The presence of Mary to Jesus was not all essentially in the order of the flesh, even though it was established on the level of the Incarnation. It was a presence of the order of faith and of supernatural love.

The presence of Mary is prolonged in an analogous manner in the life of the mystical Christ, the Church. This presence is not primarily in the order of the emotions but in the order of the virtues— faith, hope, and love. It is based on a careful attention to what is really Mary's place in the mysteries of the life of Christ and in the communion of saints: a full and universal participation in the mystery of salvation.

Mary's presence is not of the same order as that of Christ, either in the natural order or in the supernatural order. Christ is present as the Word "in whom all things were made" and in whom everything subsists. If He should cease to actuate our existence, we would cease to be. But Mary's presence does not actuate our existence.

Jesus is present to us as the principle in the order of grace. He immediately activates our souls. Mary is not the source of creation and existence or of grace, for she is entirely dependent on this order. Mary receives from Him all that she does for us. It is in Him that she loves us and in Him that her motherly care reaches out to us.

The mystery of the Incarnation gives meaning to Mary's twofold presence in the mystery of salvation: her presence before God and her presence among men. The two utterances spoken at Cana find their meaning with God and with men. The first is addressed to Jesus, telling him of man's thirst: "They have no wine"; the second is addressed to men, telling them to hope for God's gift and to do His will: "Do whatever he tells you."

Mary's presence in the Church, among the members of Christ, means that she exercises an influence over them in regard to the apostolate. Pope Paul VI stressed the point in this fashion—

> Devotion to the Blessed Virgin . . . will teach you to center all things in Christ, her divine Son, and to cultivate the interior life and essential condition for the apostolate, even through the common and daily solicitudes of life. Such a devotion will also give you continuous inspiration to be generous, humble, and ardent collaborators of our Lord Jesus Christ for the salvation of souls. What else is the apostolate if not this—to live and spend oneself for the Lord, in the constant irradiation that promotes good around us. This has been the apostolate of Mary most holy, to the most sublime and intense degree, never ceasing, not even from heaven where she prays incessantly that the fruits of the Redemption will be continually applied and extended to the Church and to humanity. [Nov. 26, 1966]

Renè Laurentin thinks that the concept of Mary as the ideal of woman is undergoing a change today, civilization has changed so much in the past few years and woman's role has undergone such a transition and transformation. Mary was considered a kind of ideal image because of her purity and humility. He thinks that most women today do not find themselves in this image. "The situation of the woman had not changed at all between the first centuries of the Judæo-Christian era and the beginning of our own century. Women were doing almost the same jobs, sewing, cooking and cleaning. A woman's economic and civil rights were inferior to those of men. . . . She had little or no access to intellectual culture, schooling, the liberal professions. She was reduced to what the Germans called the three K's: *Kinder, Küche, Kirche*—children, kitchen, church."

Mary was a "psychological model of an eternal minor living in the shadow of man in an underdeveloped situation in a civilization which was itself underdeveloped . . . Mary is no longer a material model for woman. One can no longer subject the woman to the image of Mary in the measure in which she is a witness of a state of civilization which has been surpassed. . . . She remains the woman who knew how to take to herself in God the universality of the world . . . in the particular historical situation which was here, by receiving Christ and giving him birth. The situation is no longer the same, but the manner in which the Virgin knew how to accept the situation which was hers in order to receive Christ in faith remains a model."

Our Lord is the supreme and universal model for all mankind, first of all for Our Lady. It is in His humanity, not in masculinity, that He redeemed the world. Mary's pledge of virginity was not the type of incomplete or underdeveloped femininity. Her resolve not to know man was not a withdrawal from sexuality but a transcending of it.

While the Laurentin comment is interesting, perhaps it is not wholly valid. There have been rapid changes in society and social structure indeed, and women have assumed new roles—in economics, politics, the professions. But woman's essential role has not changed, nor has human nature. The virtues of womanhood resplendent in Mary are still needed in human society—her purity, humility, her service of others—and most of all her faith, her love, and her union with Christ. Jesus is the primary model, and Mary is a secondary model, for all men and women.

Perhaps the most relevant concept for Our Lady at the present time is in terms of sign. We have long used the word in reference to the sacraments; now we also say that Christ is the sacrament of God, manifesting Him to the world. The Church is the sacrament of Christ, manifesting and expressing Him to mankind. In some analogous way so also is Mary. She points the way to her Son. Perhaps the most significant text for this section of our book is the verse from the last book of the Bible, the Apocalypse: "A great sign appeared in the heaven, a woman. . . ."

Mary was a sign of Christ and of God: she externalized the divine Presence in the world. She is a sign of God's special intervention in history, not merely of His coming but of His taking a human nature with all the components of man. Mary is a sign of the Incarnation of the Word. It is through her that He enters human history. He comes directly through her, and she stands before the world as proof that He is not some kind of apparition, not a spirit, but real among the very creatures He has made.

Mary's consent to the heavenly messenger brought the Word into His universe in a manner which changed the entire course of history. Mary's role is not a kind of exuberance of sentimentalism but is rooted in the revealed word of God and in the salvation history of the universe. If men lose sight of Mary as a sign, *the* special sign of Christ among men, then they will lose sight of the meaning of the Incarnation and of His birth and of the very significance of the mystery of divine law for man.

Mary has a sacramental value: she is a sign in connection with the events of the Lord's suffering and death. She gave Him the flesh that was maltreated and disfigured by puny men who thought they had overcome the Saviour of the world. The bone of her bone and flesh of her flesh hung upon the cross as the redemptive offering to the Father, to heal the breach of separation, to make men at one with God again in the mystery of the Atonement.

Mary was a sign to the apostles and to the world as she stood erect at the foot of the cross, the perfect *orans,* pray-er, as she was inseparably united with Him in this mystery of love and suffering. Mary is the woman of all history, because she is the mother of Jesus and because she was inseparably associated with Him in the salvation of the world. Her spiritual motherhood was ratified from the podium of the cross for all the world to hear, a treasure that Christians should appreciate so deeply.

But Mary did not simply suffer because of Jesus. She is a sign of the efficacy of that sacrifice and that love. She was redeemed too—as Franciscan doctors have longed to tell us—and as the Church proclaimed more than a century ago—by the merits of her Son and Saviour. Mary is the sign of the inner elevation of grace: "Hail, full of grace, the Lord is with you."

Mary is a sign of the elevation of grace given to a creature. St. Ambrose said that on Calvary, Mary rejoiced, not in the suffering of her Son but because the world was being saved. Mary is a sign of the power of the resurrection of Christ. Did He appear to her after He rose from the dead? We are not certain, but we may suppose that He did. We know that she was taken to heaven, "the first fruits of those who sleep," in dignity and love. Mary shared in His advent into the world, and she shared too in His redemptive act; and she shared in His victory over sin, death, and hell.

Mary is the woman in heaven, crowned with twelve stars, the moon at her feet. She is a sign before the Church and the world that men do not have a lasting city but seek one that is to come. She has attained the end of the pilgrimage, but the rest of mankind must seek for it by the grace of Christ. "I will not leave you orphans," Jesus said at the Last Supper to the apostles. No, He would send the Holy Spirit; He would also give His mother to encompass the world. Mary is a sign that men have a destiny beyond the grave, that they are destined for glory forever in paradise. Mary is a sign to our nuclear world of the primacy of spiritual values and enduring realities which no earthly power can destroy or take away. The pilgrim people of God are on the march toward their eternal homeland, not wandering, not disheartened, but full of faith and of love, like Mary, in seeking for the goal of all striving and longing. Mary is a sign in the heaven toward which we can reach out with our hands and with our hearts for the fulfillment that will never die or diminish.

Mary is the sign of the completion of human personality in all its aspects. She is a sign that though the mystery of salvation must be lived in faith and suffering, as well as in the liturgy, the kingdom of God has been established. It began on earth in the Incarnation and will continue, perfected forever, in heaven.

Mary is a sign of the victory of Christ in each of His followers. The battle continues and will do so until the end of the world, but victory is man's just as certain as it was for Our Lady. Mary is the sign of the power of prayer. She is capable of the most loving intercession because she loved most fully and believed most deeply. Mary's union with Christ on earth is deepened and intensified in heaven. She is not merely a holy woman associated with Jesus; she is a mighty sign of the humanity of God. Her relationship to Christ is as essential as His own flesh, and that was essential for human redemption, for the Father decreed that the Word should be "enfleshed" in the world.

On a side altar of the Basilica of St. Peter in Rome stands the incomparable statue of the *Pietà* by Michelangelo. The two figures are part of the whole; it is impossible to separate one from the other without destroying the total masterpiece. So the masterpiece of God's love—the mystery of salvation wrought by Jesus—cannot be violated or distorted. Mary and Jesus are inseparable, not because they are equal but because in the providence and mercy of God the Incarnate Word and His mother are together woven into the fabric of human history and because she stands beside Him and with Him in the victory of God over the foolishness of men. Mary is the sign of Christ: she is the Mother of the Church. She lives forever in the heaven of the redeemed and in the hearts of her children on earth

In an article, "Mary: Sign of Unity," Dr. Pelikan said that Mary should be a sign of unity for Christians and for all the world. "Of this family and these relations, the Blessed Virgin is the sign. As she is the first to believe in Christ the Incarnate One, and as she is represented in the New Testament throughout, she stands for our unity in the family of God. Her faithful obedience and hope are shared by all believers in Christ, regardless of whether or not they are willing

to pay her reverence. Like the beloved disciple, we find ourselves in a new family, because of Christ, partaking of a new
unity and looking for an even deeper union with God and
with one another."

In the Credo (June 30, 1968) Pope Paul VI affirmed the
traditional belief of the Church in the Virgin Mary—

> We believe that Mary is the Mother, who remained ever a virgin, of
> the Incarnate Word, our God and Saviour Jesus Christ, and that by
> reason of this singular election, she was, in consideration of the
> merits of her Son, redeemed in a more eminent manner, preserved
> from all stain of original sin and filled with the gift of grace more
> than all other creatures.
>
> Joined by a close and indissoluble bond to the mysteries of the
> Incarnation and Redemption, the Blessed Virgin, the Immaculate,
> was at the end of her earthly life raised body and soul to heavenly
> glory and likened to her risen Son in anticipation of the future lot
> of all the just; and we believe that the Blessed Mother of God,
> the New Eve, the Mother of the Church, continues in heaven her
> maternal role with regard to Christ's members, cooperating with the
> birth and growth of divine life in the souls of the redeemed.

Christ is the center of all life, but in the refulgence of
that glow stands Our Lady, who brings Him to the world
and is the motherly center of unity for the entire Christian
family. Mary is the center for all men of every religious persuasion. Father Charles Boyer, S.J., president of the Unitas
Association in Rome, has thus written of Mary—

> The intention of the council in speaking of the Mother of God
> has been in general, understood: to maintain and to reaffirm the
> doctrine commonly accepted, without establishing new definitions
> and taking into consideration in the expressions used the sensibili-
> ties of Protestants in this regard. The insertion of Marian doctrine
> into the schema of the Church was well received. The positive
> purpose relating to this insertion, namely, to illustrate the intimate
> relationship between Mary and the Church has been retained. It
> is to be noted in this connection that a relative majority in the
> voting was attained only after it had been stated that any diminu-
> tion of the privileges of the Virgin Mary was excluded. Considering
> Mary as the most eminent member of the Church, the council, as

Pastor Herbert Roux acknowledges, "has in no way intended to minimize the place of Mary or reduce the importance of the Marian doctrines promulgated." [*Réforme*, Aug. 15, 1964.]

The theologians who would have wished a deep insight into Marian doctrine will continue their studies and at an opportune time their efforts will meet with appreciation. In the meanwhile, Protestants can observe how Catholics who honor the Mother of the Saviour are not therefore hindered from adoring and serving her Son. In fact, Dr. Roux himself affirms that without the gospel testimony of Mary, the perfect knowledge of Christ would be lacking. [*Unitas*, xvi, 270]

The Blessed Virgin Mary, immaculately conceived, full of grace, associated with her Son in the salvation of the world, is not only the Mother of God but also the Mother of the Church. She is the loving mother of all the redeemed, because she is the mother of Jesus, redeemer of all men. Mary is the type, the image, the model and most eminent and perfect member of the Church. Like the Church, with the Church, and in the Church, Mary leads men with motherly solicitude and prayer to union with her divine Son. She is the way to Christ; she enables men to attain salvation and to enjoy its precious reward. She leads the way to her Son and to the final beauty, unity, and love of heaven.

> Holy Mary, Mother of the Church,
> Mother of Unity,
> Pray for all your children upon earth.
> Join them together in unity;
> Give them faith, courage and unfailing love;
> Bring them to the fullness of joy, peace,
> HOLINESS, AND BEAUTY, IN PARADISE. AMEN.

BIBLIOGRAPHY

BOOKS

Alastruey, S. *The Blessed Virgin Mary*. St. Louis, 1963.

Balic, C. *De Maria et Oecononismo*. Rome, 1965.

Bernard, R. *Mystery of Mary*. St. Louis, 1960.

Bouyer, L. *Seat of Wisdom*. New York, 1962.

———. *Woman and Man with God*. London, 1962.

Box, H. S., and Mascall, E. L., eds. *The Blessed Virgin Mary: Essays by Anglican Writers*. London, 1963.

Cantinant, J. *Mary in the Bible*. Westminster, Md., 1965.

Cranny, T. *Our Lady and Reunion*. Peekskill, N.Y., 1962.

Cutler, H., ed. *Religious Situation 1968*. Boston, 1968.

Daniel-Rops, H. *The Book of Mary*. Garden City, N.Y., 1963.

Feiner, J., Trutsch, J., and Bockle, F. *Theology Today*. Milwaukee, 1965.

Flanagan, D. *The Evolving Church*. Dublin, 1966.

Flannery, A. *Vatican II: The Constitution on the Church*. Dublin, 1966.

Galot, J. *Mary in the Gospel*. Westminster, Md., 1965.

Garofalo, S. *Mary in the Bible*. Milwaukee, 1961.

Graef, H. *Devotion to the Blessed Virgin*. London, 1963.

———. *Mary: A History of Doctrine and Devotion*. 2 vols. London, 1963, 1966.

Habig, Marion, O.F.M. *Marian Era*. Vols. 1-8. Chicago.

Laurentin, R. *Mary and the Mass*. New York, 1960.

———. *The Place of Mary*. Westminster, Md., 1966.

———. *Queen of Heaven*. Dublin, 1966.

———. *La vierge au concile*. Paris, 1965.

Lawson, J. *Ireneic Mariology*, Peekskill, N. Y., 1967.

Lubac, H. de. *Splendor of the Church*. New York, 1956. See espec. chap. "The Church and Our Lady."

Marian Library Studies. University of Dayton, Dayton, Ohio.

McNamara, K., ed. *Mother of the Redeemer*. New York, 1960.

O'Meara, T. A. *Mary in Protestant and Catholic Theology*. New York, 1966.

Patsch, J. *Our Lady in the Gospels*. London, 1958.

Rahner, H. *Mary and the Church*. New York, 1961.

———. *Our Lady and the Church*. London, 1961.

Rahner, K. *Mary, Mother of the Lord*. London, 1962.

Russell, R., Wakefield, G., and de Satge, J. C. *Mother of Jesus*. Reprint from *One in Christ*, 1968, chap. 2.

Scheeben, M. J. *Mariology*. 2 vols. St. Louis, 1946-47.

Schillebeeck, ed. *Mary, Mother of the Redemption*. London, 1964.

Semmelroth, O. *Mary, Archetype of the Church*. New York, 1964.

Suenens, L. J. *Mary, Mother of God*. London, 1959.

———. *Theology of the Apostolate*. Techay, Ill., 1962.

Thurian, M. *Mary, Mother of the Saviour*. Trans. from the French. New York, 1965.

Vigmiler. *Commentary on Vatican II*. London, 1968.

Vollert, C. *Theology of Mary*. Westminster, Md., 1965.

Vorgrimler, H. *Commentary on the Documents of Vatican II*. 6 vols. London, 1968-70.

Ward, M. *Documents of Dialogue*. Englewood, N. J., 1966

Weiger, J. *Mary, Mother of Our Faith*. London, 1960.

ARTICLES

Ahern, B. "Mary, Prototype of the Church," *New Horizons* (Notre Dame, Ind.), 1963.

Balic, Charles., O.F.M. "Mary and Vatican II," Peekskill, 1966.

Burghardt, W., S.J. "Mary and Reunion," *Catholic Mind*, Jan., 1962.

———. "Mary, Obstacle to Reunion," *Ecumenism and Vatican II.* Milwaukee, 1964.

Butler, C. "Marian Doctrine Seen as Uniting, Not Dividing Christians," *Unitas,* 1963.

Cranny, T. "Pope Paul and Our Lady," *Marian Era,* Chicago, 1966.

Deikmann, G. "Mary, Model of Our Worship," *Come Let Us Worship.* Baltimore, 1961.

Durwell, F. X. "Mary Amongst Us," *In the Redeeming Christ.* New York, 1963.

Hamer, J. "Mary and Protestants," *Worship,* Nov. 1963.

Hurley, M. "Ecumenism and Mariology: Contribution of Catholics," *Furrow,* 1963.

———. "Ecumenism and Mariology: Contribution of Protestants," *Furrow,* 1964.

O'Conoughe, N. D. "Mary and the Church," in *What Is the Church?* ed. D. Flanagan. Glen Rock, N. J., 1962.

Pocock, P. "Mary in the Church," *Ecumenist,* 1964.

Sartory, T. "Does Christ's Mother Divide Us?" *Theology Digest,* Vol. 12 (1964).

Vaughan, A. "Development of Marian Doctrine as an Ecumenical Problem," *Marian Studies,* Vol. 15 (1964).